D1271626

BRUMBACK LIBRARY

3 3045 00053 1687

745.5
B78p

c.1

WITHDRAWN

THE BRUMBACK LIBRARY
OF VAN WERT COUNTY
VAN WERT, OHIO

PIÑATAS

by Virginia Brock

illustrations by
Anne Marie Jauss

745.5
B 78 p

ABINGDON
Nashville

Piñatas
Seventh Printing 1977
Copyright © 1966 by Abingdon Press
All Rights Reserved
Printed in the United States of America
ISBN 0-687-31436-4
Library of Congress Catalog Card Number: 66-10567

To my family
Brocky, Dale, Jim, David, and Bonnie

c. 1

11/28/80 B&J

CONTENTS

Pignattas of the type in use in
Italy in the sixteenth century

Photographs by *Borchi* used
through the courtesy of *MUSEO
INTERNAZIONALE DELLE
CERAMICHE*, Faenza, Italy

HOW THE PIÑATA BEGAN

Wouldn't it seem strange to decorate Easter eggs on Halloween? Give Valentines at Christmas? Or trim a Christmas tree on the Fourth of July? That is because each festive day has its own special objects and traditions.

But there is one object which can be a part of all of these holidays and festivals: the *piñata!* Filled to the brim with candy or surprise gifts and adorned with colored paper, it can add joy and gaiety to almost any occasion.

Since its origin in Italy its use throughout the world has come to signify warmth, friendliness, and festiveness. It is especially fun to think of a *piñata* as a treasure chest. Hidden within its petals, cones, and gilded trappings may lie treasures of great variety. Most of us have seen beautiful *piñatas* that look like birds, pineapples, flowers, or silver stars. But the *piñatas* of 400 years ago were as different from those of today as a sticker weed is different from a lily.

In the early part of the sixteenth century, the Italian people were living in a historical period called the Renaissance. They began to give more consideration to themselves and less thought to the church. Pleasures and amusements became more important to them.

Only the wealthy learned to read and write. For amusement the people relied heavily upon their own wits. They invited guests to their homes and played guessing games in which their memories were tested rigorously. They told entertaining stories. Most of them portrayed roles in plays and skits.

Some of the games involved the playing of tricks upon a blindfolded person. In one such game a pineapple-shaped clay pot was suspended in the air by a cord, swung about, then broken with a stick. The earthenware pot was called a *pignatta*, which comes from the Italian word *pigna* meaning cone-shaped.

It was the nature of the *pignatta* to be destroyed, and few relics remain. We can only guess at the contents of a sixteenth-century *pignatta*, but it is exciting to imagine that sometimes among the more usual sweets there may have been hidden a formula for a magic potion or a map to an underground city or a secret plea for rescue from an evil captor.

By the middle of the sixteenth century, Italian ideas and customs had filtered to other countries in Europe. Many Italian adventurers, lured by the warm climate of Spain, went there and took with them their *pignatta* custom. The Italian word *pignatta* was now changed to the Spanish word *piñata*.

In Spain the atmosphere was less gay. It was a somber time of religious severity. Long at war with the non-Christian Moors, the Spanish people gave religious significance to almost every occasion. They designated the first Sunday of Lent as *Piñata* Sunday. They practiced the festive custom of breaking the *piñata* only during Lent. Referred to as *Pascua de Cuaresma*, it was and still is a period of fast and penance. On

10

that day, throughout Spain, the people donned black masks and held a masquerade ball. Whether they danced the *bolero,* the *flamenco,* or the *zarabanda,* the ball was called the Dance of the *Piñata.* During the dance a *piñata* was broken. In the nineteenth century, the Spanish writer Juan Martinez Villergos wrote a novel about it called *The Dance of the Piñata.*

The Spanish word *piñata* referred to the game itself rather than to the clay jug. The *piñata* container, which was used ordinarily for food and water, was called an *olla.* It was squat and round and, like the Italian jug, it was left rough, undecorated, and unglazed by the potters. It was indeed homely; and some Spanish people concealed its ugliness by building a figure around the clay pot.

While its popularity has somewhat waned in Spain, it has gained momentum throughout the Americas. We have no recorded arrival of the *piñata* to the shores of Mexico, but there is little doubt that it was carried by some of the Spanish explorers almost 400 years ago. Most of the explorers who came to Mexico were eager to spread Spanish culture and religion.

In Mexico the *piñata* continued to have religious significance but it underwent several changes. One involved the time of its use. Whereas in Spain it was associated with the Lenten season, the *piñata* in Mexico is also a traditional Christmas-time festivity. It is as familiar there as the decorated Christmas tree is in the United States. The word *pascua,* signifying a church holiday, may have been interpreted in the New World to refer only to the Christmas season. Possibly a fun-loving Spanish sailor initiated the *piñata* game in Mexico, or an account of the *piñata* custom may have been exchanged quite desperately for a life during an encounter with the Indians.

The appearance of the *piñata* has undergone a more elaborate change. As recently as twenty-five or thirty years ago the *piñata,* aside from very simple ornamentation, was plainly a clay jar. Then, with the availability of China paper, or tissue paper, the Mexicans began to decorate *piñatas* to look like carrots, roses, pineapples, and even radishes.

When large numbers of tourists from the United States traveled throughout Mexico, another important change occurred. Enchanted with the custom, the tourists wished to buy more *piñatas* than the potters could supply. The manufacturers, eager to increase their income, sought a faster method of making *piñatas;* so they made them of *papier-mâché.* It was found they could quickly make figures of bulls, stars, donkeys, ducks, and many others. A *piñata* is seldom made in the realistic likeness of a person.

Thousands of *piñatas* are made, filled, and broken for the Christmas season alone, though that is only one among many occasions when they are used: Some families buy them from the marketplaces or the village *piñata* maker. Many more make their own, frequently at *piñata*-making parties. Sometimes two or three families bring goodies for the *piñata*. In the U. S. it probably would be called a "pot luck *piñata."*

Even now some families continue to use as the base of the *piñata* a clay pot or jar. Before the *piñata*-making event someone in the family makes a large clay jar. It is baked in an oven hot enough to fuse the clay but not so hot that the jar will emerge hard and glass-like. It must be a jar that can be broken easily. When the jar is taken from the oven and cooled, the family gives its *piñata*-making party.

On the day of the party pastries are baked in large quantities to serve the guests. Not only will the immediate family take part in the *piñata*-making project, but many relatives and friends may help. Today, one of the interesting tasks is deciding what kind of *piñata* to make. The finished product may be a star, a chicken, or a donkey.

Since the arrival of the custom in Mexico, traditional sweets have been used to fill the *piñata*. They include many kinds of nuts and fresh

13

limes. Sugar cane, small green apples, and the wild fruit *tejocotes* are also used. If the family can provide them, small toys or gifts are placed in the *piñata*. Among well-to-do families the treats sometimes are of an elaborate and rare nature.

A custom which is entirely Mexican in origin is the staging of *Posadas* after which a *piñata* is broken. *Posada* means inn or shelter, and the *Posadas* pageants which are enacted from the sixteenth to the twenty-fourth of December symbolize the struggle of the holy family, Mary and Joseph, to find shelter for the night.

Although the ritual has solemn religious meaning, the players—often an entire neighborhood—portray their roles with great merriment. Two people at the head of the procession carry small images of Mary and Joseph. The others carry lighted candles. As the group moves from house to house they sing the traditional songs of the *Posadas*. The songs, varying in words and music in different parts of Mexico, are a musical conversation between Joseph and an innkeeper. At each house "Joseph" sings a plea for shelter. At each house he is refused by the innkeeper with a rude "No!" When the procession moves to the last home, the conversation is repeated, but now the travelers are welcomed.

They place their lighted candles around the *nacimiento*, the nativity scene, which can be found in almost any home in Mexico at Christmas. Once the religious ceremony is completed, all attention focuses upon the breaking of the *piñata*. In some areas of Mexico a *piñata* is broken on each of the nine nights before Christmas, in others it is broken only on Christmas Eve.

If someone should be so unfortunate as not to get a gift from the *piñata*, he sings a traditional song asking the hostess to hurry out with the basket of treats. Not only does she graciously bring out more of the treats, she also gives an additional favor to each guest to carry home. The favors are usually miniature glass toys filled with candies.

14

Although the *piñata* itself has undergone changes in the four hundred years of its existence, the playing of the game has remained virtually the same.

The filled pot is suspended by a rope at a height just above arm's reach of those who will play the game. The ceiling, balcony, or limb of a tree will do very well, but it is important that the rope be strung through a hook, over a pulley, or be otherwise movable. Guests usually approach the activity with high anticipation, and it is important to allow ample "swinging room."

One guest, chosen by the party giver, is blindfolded and led to the spot beneath the *piñata*. There he is handed a broomstick, while the

others are reminded to stand a safe distance away. An important trick is to give the *piñata* a big swing so that it will be more difficult to hit. The game can be enlivened even more by giving the person a few spins before sending him careening on his way toward the *piñata*.

The guest usually takes three swings at the *piñata*, as the group sings "Jingle Bells," "Happy Birthday," "For He's a Jolly Good Fellow," or any other song appropriate to the celebration. If he is unsuccessful—and the suspense is as exciting as the actual breaking—he passes the stick and blindfold to the next guest and the game goes on until the *piñata* is broken. When the contents fall to the floor, a scrambling for the gifts begins.

16

While the *piñata* is usually depicted as an activity for youngsters, it is enjoyed fully as much by adults. Social affairs frequently begin with the breaking of a *piñata*.

Occasionally the *piñata* is used for mischievous purposes. It may be filled with objects which have a special meaning for the guests, after which a treat-filled *piñata* may follow.

In present-day Italy, in the state of Tuscany, the game has yet another variation. Three *piñatas* are commonly hung together at a time of *festas* or other social occasions. One may contain ashes, one water, and one treats. Of course, the poor blindfolded fellow can only guess in which direction to swing—and then duck.

Another variation called *pentolaccia,* is played in Italy where the treats or gifts of the pot go to the one competitor who breaks it.

While to most people the *piñata* is an object of great fun and delight, there are some who see it as a symbol of evil. As a person hits the *piñata* with a stick, a temptation is banished, and the stick wielder is rewarded with the treats.

Today, the *piñata* custom is spread among many nations including Spain, Italy, Portugal, British Honduras, Latin America, the United States, and Canada.

In some parts of the United States teachers and students often plan a *piñata* party in conjunction with the teaching program.

What is the secret of its great appeal? First, the *piñata*, as a colorful decoration, is a symbol of gaiety. Almost any party theme can be dramatized by its use. It contains the promise of a surprise. Its greatest appeal lies perhaps in its hint of hidden treasures and magic wings—a map to a fairy castle or to the cave of a one-eyed Cyclops!

Who would not become excited by such a treasure chest?

FIVE GOLD CHAINS

It was the spring of 1525. For long weeks the Spanish sailing vessel *Caravel* had labored through the rough Atlantic toward Campeche in the land of New Spain. There was not even a glimpse of land.

"Andres de Villafina," yelled Captain Guzman in a bellow that rattled his gold vest chains. "Are the horses on their feet? Are the casks holding tight?"

"Only one horse is lame, sir. The casks are secure," Andres said, standing at attention before the stout, pompous captain. What a life for a skilled seaman! Exercising stiff-jointed horses and playing nursemaid to water casks. And for an ill-tempered captain so greedy for gold that he displays not one but five gold chains on his velvet cloak.

The sky was as black as the sea. Andres and his friend Cristobal lay stretched across the wooden deck. With food supplies low, the cook had brewed an evening meal of seaweed and olive oil. Though two hours had passed since the meal, Andres felt it still tumble and slosh inside him.

18

Giant waves sprayed his arms with mist that dried in a hard salty crust.

Bumpety bump! He glanced at the cloth satchel that dangled from a wooden peg above his head. In the bottom of the bag lay the *piñata* which his mother had filled with nuts and fruits and then had lightly sealed for him to take along.

Andres, eager to begin his adventure, had sailed before *Piñata* Sunday. When Captain Guzman had explained most grandly his appointment by the court to explore New Spain, Andres agreed to sail immediately as his assistant. Now the captain spoke only of the gold which he hoped to find there.

Before Andres sailed, his mother had said sadly, "Here, Andres, since you cannot enjoy the *piñata* at home, take it with you and enjoy it wherever you are."

There was no time for *piñata* games or any other aboard the *Caravel*. Now *Piñata* Sunday had surely come and gone; yet Andres had not eaten the contents, nor could he bring himself to toss the noisome thing overboard.

So each night as he tried to sleep, the satchel bumped and bounced with the rocking rhythm of the ship. Someday perhaps he would use it.

Andres had no more than closed his eyes, it seemed, when morning came.

"Hey, Andres, you sleep as though glued to the deck!" said Cristobal as his short sturdy fingers secured a rope. "The majestic captain has begun his raving even earlier today. He's coming toward us with his fancy-feathered hat swaying this way and about!"

Andres raked his fingers through his black hair and stumbled below deck as fast as his sleep-weakened legs could find their way. The horses were waiting for him.

The captain had chosen six nearly identical animals for their chestnut coats, their broad chests, and fine legs. Each wore a shiny silver breastplate from which hung an engraved silver bell. Who knew whether the Indians of Campeche were friendly or whether they were like those of Cape Catoche who carried poisoned arrows?

Around and around the deck Andres strode, leading one horse at a time, to forecastle to stern and back again. Andres, all but dizzy, finally tethered the last horse in the small, dank hold.

The cook was setting fire to wood for the evening meal. Andres hoped he would not have to eat seaweed that night. He stooped and felt each water cask carefully. There was no sign of leaking water.

"Land, land, I see it!" came shouts from on deck. Up over the casks Andres vaulted like a long-limbed monkey. A porthole looked directly toward the west. Clinging to a ledge he saw it, the bountiful land called New Spain!

Andres turned around to go down. Now, how had he climbed up? But before he could plan a course of retreat, the pile of casks began rolling and bouncing and cracking. Andres tumbled down many times faster than he had climbed up! He pushed aside a cask and got up from the wet, moldy floor. What of his skinned shins? He was looking at a catastrophe, one which he, an able seaman, had created. At least seven of the precious casks lay with holes like gaping mouths. They first splashed, then drooled water on the floor.

The captain will surely flog me and bind me in chains, thought Andres. As he was considering his fate, the form of the raging captain seemed to fill the hold.

"De Villafina, you clod-footed bumbler!"

"The casks rolled faster than I have ever seen anything move, Captain."

The captain's tone became ominous. "And just how many casks of water remain after your clumsiness?"

Andres moved painfully to one cask, then another.

20

"Well, how many?" The captain's roar hurt Andres' ears.

"It appears we have two whole casks left, sir."

"That is barely enough to keep my crew alive till we reach Campeche. And what of my horses?"

Andres cleared his throat. "If I may make a suggestion, Captain, sir, isn't that Campeche that we see from our ship? Can't we get water there?"

Guzman's eyes glistened. "Campeche? Not yet, but there may be water there." Then he yelled to the crew: "Prepare to drop anchor!"

"Tomorrow morning, de Villafina, you will look for water on the new land and bring word to the ship." Quietly he said, "I shall even pick out a horse to carry you on your journey."

When the captain had gone, Cristobal said, "Don't go! I heard the Captain say this is not Campeche but Cape Catoche where the Indians shoot poisoned arrows."

"Surely not even Captain Guzman would send me to Cape Catoche. But what can I do?"

Cristobal looked at his friend. "I can go with you if you like."

Andres smiled at his good friend who was willing to share his danger. "There is no use in both of us risking our lives. And it was I who broke the water casks."

That night Andres counted four hundred and sixty-three bumps of the satchel against the ship.

When morning came, Guzman said, "You told me before we sailed that you yearned for adventure. I shall see that you have it!"

The captain held the reins of one of the horses. "Here you are, a fine animal." The horse stood with the sun reflecting from its silver breastplate.

"Look," whispered Cristobal. "He has given you the one lame horse."

"Gather your possessions, de Villafina. Your miserable belongings will do no one here any good."

The satchel hung from Andres' shoulder.

"If you have not succeeded in finding water and returning here by sundown, we will move on to Campeche without you."

It took several minutes for Andres to row the boat carrying himself and the lame horse to land. When they stepped into the sudsy breakers, Andres turned around and waved sadly to Cristobal. He pulled the boat up on the sand. Cape Catoche!

In the morning sunlight the new country was as bright and beautiful

as his own Spain. Together, he and the horse walked across the warm sand.

Though Andres walked to spare the horse, it limped badly. Only a small cask for water lay across the animal's back.

Young stalks of wild maize grew over the hillside; yet Andres could see no sign of water nearby. Seeing that the sun had risen directly over his head, he stopped beneath a tree. Bread made of flour and seawater lay in his satchel beside the *piñata*. Though he listened, he could hear no sounds but those which came from his limping horse.

"You poor sick beast of a horse. You froth at the mouth from thirst." His own mouth tasted of salt, and he picked up a handful of grass and sucked the juice from it.

"When the wind blows from the west, I think I can smell wet dirt. There must be water somewhere!"

Andres looked toward the ship. The red and yellow flag of Spain fluttered in the breeze. The ship was still waiting, but time was passing quickly. Andres and the horse walked on.

The sound of running water came to his ears. When he reached the top of a knoll, he saw a cold, glassy stream below. "Come on, horse," he said excitedly. "Now, we can both drink and fill the cask!"

He had no more than lifted the cask when his back was pelted in a hundred places! Tiny rocks lay about him on the ground. Almost immediately a tall Indian stood beside him.

"Why you come to Cape Catoche?" he asked slowly, as though not sure of the words.

Andres had never looked directly into the face of an Indian before. His skin was a red bronze. The muscles of his arms were broad and thick, and—Andres could not believe his eyes. Around the Indian's neck hung five gold chains, exactly like those of Captain Guzman! Many more Indians appeared from the bushes.

24

"I'm from Captain Guzman's ship," said Andres. "I came in search of water for our men and horses." Andres put his hand to his mouth as though he were drinking water.

Andres knew that some explorers, wishing to spread Spanish culture, had treated the Indians kindly. But many more, greedy for the jewels and gold of New Spain, had tortured the Indians.

"Why does your horse wear the shiny armor?" asked the big Indian angrily. He pressed the chains together. "Another who rode such a horse lies dead beyond the hills. He killed my men."

Then the gold chains were Captain Guzman's! Why had the Captain left the ship? Andres looked at the silver armor on his horse. The Indians moved nervously. Sensing their leader's anger, some lifted arrows from their slings.

"Here, I will show you. I will remove the armor."

But just as Andres moved, he was lifted roughly by the arms and carried through the air to a cottonwood tree. The Indians gathered in front of him—the men who had killed the Captain.

The weight of the satchel hung heavy on his shoulder. The *piñata*! Perhaps they would like it and forget about him, at least for a while.

"I have a great gift for you!" He made his voice sound as though he were not afraid. "Here, men of New Spain." He held the reddish, rough clay jar high above his head. Their eyes followed his movements but without interest. Truly, in appearance it was little different from their own clay jugs.

But to Andres, it suddenly became very dear. The clay had come from his own yard in Spain. The *piñata* had been filled in his own home. "It is a *piñata* of the *Pascuas*," Andres said.

The big Indian looked at the clay pot. He had known some Spanish words. Perhaps he had heard the word *Pascuas*. It was a word for the Christian seasons of Lent and Christmas. Andres could only hope.

The leader turned slowly and raised his hand toward the others.

"Here, I will show you how to do it," said Andres. Surely there would never be a better time to use the *piñata* which his mother had given him. Quickly by a cord of his satchel he suspended it from the tree limb. Then he handed a tough stick to the leader.

"Now hit it!" said Andres, gesturing to the man.

The Indian paused, then grunted and swung. The pot broke and pieces fell to the ground.

Suddenly, Andres did not want to look. What if they were not pleased with the treats from his own Spain? Worse, what if the treats had spoiled? The Indians stood grinning.

Andres saw the familiar almonds, hazelnuts, and chewy dried figs. His mother had even put in some bright coins and colored ribbons. He watched the Indians crush the nuts between their strong, white teeth.

"You are not like the man who stole from us and killed our men. You are a man of the *Pascuas*," said the big Indian. "Take water to your house that floats upon the sea. Take with you, too, a suckling pig for roasting and the fruits that grow in our country."

He mumbled *"Pascuas"* again, and some of the others tried to say the word.

Andres thanked him many times and said he would return with the crew in the morning.

The sun was dropping low in the sky when he reached the wet sand at water's edge. As he rowed the small boat toward the *Caravel*, he could see the sailors crowded anxiously on the deck to watch his return.

Cristobal grabbed him and pounded him on the back as soon as the boat was lifted to the deck. "How did you escape, Andres?"

"Do you remember that noisy *piñata* which bobbed against the side of the ship night after night? It has served us well."

26

"Did you see the Captain?" asked Cristobal. "About an hour after you left, he saw a golden, glittering object in the distance. He fastened his armor, grabbed a spear and a horse, and ordered us to lower him in a boat to the water. He has not returned."

The crew listened solemnly.

"Captain Guzman is dead," said Andres. "He was killed trying to steal from the Indians. He had killed some of their men." Andres told of seeing the five gold chains around the Indian's neck, of his own adventures with the Indians, and of their invitation to return for food and water.

"How lucky for us that you weren't killed, Andres," said Cristobal. "At least there is left among us one who is able to captain the ship toward Campeche."

"And when we reach Campeche," said Andres, "we will thank God for a safe journey and—yes, we will thank him especially for a *piñata*."

THE *HUARACHE* MAKERS

"Hey, Shorty, this bus is moving out . . . you coming?"

Shorty, indeed. Didn't the driver know he was speaking to *Señor* Mario Montaña, who at almost eighteen was the head of the Montaña family? Mario gripped the roll of leather hides and hopped in the bus, barely escaping the snap of the doors. He found two empty seats, one for the costly hides and one for himself. Since his father's death, Mario had operated the family's *huarache*-making business. He made purchases and decisions as he believed his father would have made them.

But some of his many relatives said, "Mario does not speak with authority as his father did . . . as his cousin Rolph does. Mario is too easy-going for an important job. And he is such a small man."

Mario sank into the bus seat as he rode out of the big city. It did not feel at all like Christmas Eve. His feet burned. He had looked everywhere, but he had not been able to find his sister Carmella.

Three days ago he had commanded his sister to walk in the *Posadas*, the traditional procession when families and friends walk from house to house asking for shelter for the holy family, Mary and Joseph. Mario had commanded his sister, surely as his father would have done, Mario told himself, and what had she done? She had run away.

His relatives had said that if Carmella did not return and walk in the *Posadas* on Christmas Eve, Rolph should be made head of the family. And now Mario was returning from the city without Carmella. He had not found her.

It had been three days before Christmas when it all happened. Mario's mother had come to the workshop door and said, "Mario, you must speak to your sister. She is talking against the *Posadas*. You know if our relatives hear of it they will say Rolph should be head of our family. He is a strict one."

The relatives would soon arrive to make the red and white radish *piñata* which they would break on Christmas Eve. It was a tradition they had observed each year for as long as any of them could remember.

Mario found his sister at work in the small kitchen. Boca Boca, the parrot, perched on Carmella's shoulders, was screaming, "Save me! Save me!" It was a noisy bird, and Mario tolerated it only because Carmella loved it.

Carmella, three years younger than Mario, recently had begun to criticize her home, the village, and the *huarache* business. Today, even the old, treasured custom of the *Posadas* was being attacked. Carmella had always asked questions. "Why do we do this?" she always wanted to know. "Why do we do that?" She was not like the other members of the Montaña family who lived happily by the habits and customs of their ancestors.

Today in the little kitchen she was dropping pale blobs of seed cooky dough on a pan, then furiously pounding each blob with her fist.

Mario felt great tenderness toward his little sister. "I'm glad to see you are helping with the party, Carmella." He patted her shoulder gently.

"Isn't this fun, Mario? Getting up before the sun, breathing black smoke to make the fire flame, just for a *piñata* party? Just for a lot of aunts and uncles and cousins? But I'm helping. Everyone says, 'Don't ask questions, Carmella. Just work, Carmella.'"

Angry tears splashed on her blouse.

"It isn't so bad, Carmella. Look. You've only a few cookies to make. And Alfredo probably will come over to see you as usual." Alfredo was a year or two older than Carmella, and his affection for her had begun several months ago.

Mario tried to make his voice sound firm: "Then, we will all walk in the *Posadas.*"

Carmella had looked down at the rough wooden floor. She shook her head. "You will walk in the *Posadas* without me."

When Carmella had refused to talk with him any more, Mario had gone on through the house, nailing a board here, fastening a window there. He had checked the food cellar once more. There was enough food to feed them all winter.

The Montaña house was filling, now, with aunts, uncles, and cousins, including Rolph, whose hair curled tightly around his ears. Now children played in the workshop where their parents made *huaraches* during the day. Older people talked gaily and laughed loudly. One of the uncles plucked his guitar in the kitchen. At least half a dozen burros brayed or dozed at the tethering post by the kitchen door.

While Mario's mother served seed cookies and cinnamon tea, some of the relatives cut strips of colored paper for the *piñata.*

Mario stood silent and solemn. He answered the questions the family asked him. He told his uncle how many pairs of *huaraches* he had sold last month and how many *pesos* he had spent. He told his aunt how many eggs their flock of hens had laid.

30

Without looking up Mario knew that Alfredo had arrived and was standing beside him. Alfredo was a tall friendly boy who worked as a coffee bean sorter, and about him there was the unmistakable fragrance of coffee.

"Where's Carmella?" Alfredo asked.

"She's here somewhere, Alfredo."

In a lower voice, Mario confided to the boy, "She says she will not walk with the *Posadas,* but let's hope she doesn't mean it."

Mario remembered he had not seen Carmella since she was smashing the cookie dough. If she were really at the party, surely he could see her. Even among so many people, she would gleam like a beautiful jewel. Quietly, Mario slipped away and walked down to the village.

The woman who sold baskets had seen Carmella. "She got on the bus," the woman told Mario. "The bus goes to the city."

Mario walked slowly back to his home and the party. He would have to tell his mother.

"I was afraid this would happen," said his mother. "You do not have the right way with her, Mario. She has no respect."

"But I have tried to do as my father would have done," he said. "Surely, she will come back. She has very little money, I know."

His mother looked very worried and anxious, but she said, "Let us keep it between the two of us. She will come back."

Mario tried to act as though he were not worried. His mother continued to serve cookies and cinnamon tea. But the relatives knew Carmella was not among them, and there was low talking between Mario's grandparents and Rolph.

The room became quiet as Rolph stood up and walked toward Mario. "A boy who has just come from the village says Carmella has run away to the city."

Mario wished Rolph would not stand practically head to shoulder with him. He had to look up at him. "She has gone away to the city."

The relatives looked knowingly at one another, and the grandmother said, "The girl should be locked up. It is too bad her father is not alive. She needs a firm hand."

Rolph stepped forward and spoke in a loud voice: "We all like little Mario. It is too bad he does not command the Montaña family with more authority; but then he is small for a job of such importance." Rolph snapped his fingers and a small cousin brought him a cup of tea.

When Mario tried to make his voice sound as deep as Rolph's, it sounded only as if he had a cold. But he was still head of the family and the family listened.

"Since my father's death we have made enough *huaraches* to buy a milk goat and ten ducks. There has been enough work for all of us. I've fastened palm branches over our roof to keep us dry during the rains, and I have taken the young children to school. I've tried to do as my father did."

"But Carmella," Rolph began.

"With Carmella, I wish I had more wisdom." Even though the weather was damp and chill, Mario was perspiring. At night as he lay in bed he liked to remember all the things he had done since he had been head of the family. Now, standing before his relatives, he could remember only a few things.

The family looked at Rolph, tall and important, and then at Mario. Finally, an uncle got up. "Let's say that if Carmella does not return and walk in the last *Posadas* on Christmas Eve, it is proof that Mario has not done a good job. Carmella has said things against our family business, our way of life, and our village. If she goes so far as to stay away from our *Posadas,* then Mario is not a wise head of the Montaña family, no matter how many *huaraches* he has sold, and no matter if the workshop is a part of this house." The uncle then turned to Rolph, who towered above the

33

heads of his relatives like a ruler over his subjects. Everyone was quiet.

"I'm sure Carmella will come home—come home tonight," said Mario's mother. She wept as she spoke. Boca Boca fluttered a storm of yellow feathers about the room.

When the last of the relatives had gone, Mario walked again to the village. He would go to the city to search for Carmella.

Mario was coming home now—without Carmella. As he often did when he took the bus from the city, Mario kept his eyes on the crest of the pine-covered mountain. As the bus whined up the road toward the village, the little houses seemed to spring from the bushes. By the time he got home, his relatives would have gathered again to begin the last of the *Posadas,* and Rolph already would be preparing to assume his duties as head of the Montaña family.

When he unlatched the wooden door and walked in, the radish *piñata* hung from the ceiling before him. In the middle of the main room, a crowd of relatives had gathered. As he squeezed his way through the people he saw his mother, and beside her stood—Carmella!

"Carmella! Carmella!" Mario's voice was weak with excitement. "How long have you been here? How did you get here?"

Between tears and laughter, Carmella told how she had spent the time away. She had waited in the bus station in the city until the sun came up. Then she had walked all around the city, admiring the beauty of the parks and gardens. But she had been afraid and lonesome, and she had no money. The second night she had earned her lodging by helping an old lady fire clay pots in a kiln.

Carmella smiled. "She was making pots to be used in *piñatas*. It

34

seemed so strange—there were no Montañas there, but I couldn't get away from the *piñatas*. Even the *piñatas* seemed strange because they were being made to sell."

"How did you get home?" Mario interrupted.

"The woman who made the *piñatas* had friends who were coming this way. They brought me." Carmella looked very tired. She was gray from the smoke of the kiln, and a small white blister rose on the back of her hand.

Mario clenched his fists. No longer would he ask, "What would my father have done?" Nor would he ask, "Will my relatives think I am doing the right thing?" He would try another way in the short time he had left as head of the Montaña family. Mario stood beside his sister. He held up his hand to quiet the group, and then he spoke firmly and evenly:

"Carmella, you have been most unhappy and therefore have run away from your home. I think it is time we listened to those things which make you want to leave us."

Never had Carmella been asked to speak her thoughts. Mario realized for the first time that the family had always said, *"Don't ask so many questions, Carmella. Never mind, Carmella, it is our way. We have always done it. Don't ask why, Carmella."*

Carmella spoke timidly at first. "About the *huaraches*, Mario. Could we make a different kind—one that fits the foot better? Maybe one that doesn't make such a clacking noise when we walk?"

The women in the room looked down at their own feet in their *huaraches*. They were rough and calloused in the loose, floppy shoes.

"Do you have an idea for making them, Carmella?"

She nodded her head.

"Suppose you make a picture of one we could make in our shop. Certainly it would be only wise to make *huaraches* that are comfortable, attractive, and still sell for a fair price," Mario said with authority.

"And what do you dislike about the village?" Mario continued.

"Sometimes I feel," said Carmella, "that the world is going by without me. I'd like sometimes to go to the city where there are movies, buildings with pictures on them, music, parks, and beautiful stores!"

Some of the Montaña family nodded as Carmella spoke. A few had even been as far as the city.

"It is true," said Mario, "that we in the village know only one way of life. Perhaps we can bring from the city ways that will make our own lives better. And when there is shopping to be done, those who wish can take turns at going to the city. It is not right for only one to make all the trips."

The relatives smiled as if they were going on a long ocean voyage.

Carmella moved toward the *piñata*. Her friend Alfredo walked with her and held her hand. The family became silent because it was about the *piñata* and the *Posadas* that they had the deepest feelings. Most of them held tightly to the white candles they would carry in the procession.

"Must we always make a radish *piñata*? Year after year? There are flowers and animals and other lovely shapes that would be fun to make."

The relatives, and even Mario and his mother, looked at the radish *piñata* as though seeing it for the first time.

"We have always done it, Carmella," Mario said. "Of course, we don't even have to have one if we don't want to. Nor do we have to hold the *Posadas* if we choose not to." He knew he would see expressions of shock on the faces of many, but he continued, "It is a good thing we have someone like Carmella who questions these things we've done all our lives, even customs like the *piñata* and *Posadas*. Sometimes by just talking about a thing we understand it better and treasure it more."

Carmella asked, "You mean I don't have to walk in the *Posadas* unless I want to?"

Mario knew that his job as head of the Montaña family would rest on her decision, but he said quietly, "Not if it has no meaning for you."

Carmella ran her fingers lightly over the petals of the bright red radish *piñata*. The relatives, their faces softer and kinder, passed a burning candle among one another, lighting their own from it.

"Did anyone save candles for Alfredo and me?" Carmella asked.

Mario smiled as his mother handed candles to Carmella and Alfredo.

For once, Boca Boca sat quietly without screaming, "Save me! Save me!"

And for that, too, *Señor* Mario Montaña, almost eighteen and head of the Montaña family, was most thankful.

PEBBLES OF SAL AGUA

The shallow bay pointed a blue finger at the Mexican village of Sal Agua. In the water a small boat bobbed with the sea swells. At first, it appeared that Miguel was not aboard, only his father who sat waiting for a fish to snap at the hook.

If all of Miguel was not on board, at least the lower half of him clung by the toes to the inside of the boat. His head and arms trailed over the stern, and strands of his black hair skimmed the water, cutting a neat trough.

"Miguel, sit up," said his father. "Just for once let me see that you are not such a lazy one. The day is half gone and we haven't even a tail or a fin of a fish for dinner!"

Miguel secured his position with his toes and pulled his upper body into the boat. How quickly the time had passed! Never did he tire of looking at the glittering pebbles that paused to rest between the tides. He took the other fishing pole and, shivering, slid to the bottom of the boat where the brilliant December sun would dry the goose bumps from his arms. As usual the pockets of his trousers were wet and bursting with pebbles he had scooped from the water.

"Miguel," someone was calling.

Miguel and his father looked toward the beach. What was his mother doing there? She was waving a black shawl. Her loose cotton skirts blew about her ankles, whipping pinches of dust into the air. She seldom became so excited as to run down to the beach. It was at least a mile from home.

They rowed back quickly. Miguel's father secured the boat from the pull of the tides; and while his mother ran toward them, Miguel watched the sand crabs bubble and burrow for cover in the sand.

"*Señor* Morales wants you, Miguel! You are needed at the village," said his mother. "Our own *padre* is coming and he'll be here Christmas Eve, the night of the *piñata* party."

Though she had become a heavy woman, she still wore the dainty gold hoop earrings for which her ears had been pierced when she was a child.

"It's good news, Mother, but what has it to do with me, and at this moment?"

"We listened to *Señor* Morales this morning. He said the mission building is too ugly for a new *padre* to see. It must be made beautiful before he arrives."

Miguel remembered the cracks in the mission that spread like a spider's web and the wall that crumbled in his hand like meal. It was an important building to Sal Agua. The people used it for weddings, funerals and *fiestas*. Sometimes a *padre* would visit from a nearby village.

"Almost everyone has promised *Señor* Morales to help mend the cracks, but he says you are the only one in Sal Agua who can make a beautiful picture on the walls."

40

Miguel knew his mother was looking at him anxiously. Nor did she fail to see that he carted home still more pebbles to add to those which he already had.

"You know how everyone likes the glass pictures you have made, Miguel," she said.

It was true. Many people said, "Miguel has made his parents' house the most beautiful in the village."

"Now go quickly for once, Miguel," said his father, giving him a friendly shove.

His thick-soled *huaraches* made a dull clomping sound on the road. He put his hands in his pockets to keep the pebbles from bouncing out. He liked the feel of them. Some were small and slick like hummingbirds' eggs. Others felt flat and pinpricked by a hundred cactus needles.

Miguel's house was at the end of the village. He emptied the pebbles in a jar. In front of the house grew a large *tejecote* tree. The fruit hung like ripe apples from its branches, a sure sign that it was time for the *Posadas*. Beginning tomorrow night, the village would hold a candlelight procession for the nine days before Christmas, and on Christmas Eve, everyone would gather at the mission and break a beautiful *piñata*. It was the happiest time of the year.

In the center of Sal Agua stood the mission, and directly across from the mission lived *Señor* Morales. Miguel did not really call *Señor* Morales a friend. He was broad and thick with rough, stumpy hands. Wiry hair grew crookedly above his upper lip, and only one side of his mouth smiled. Almost everyone in the village listened to *Señor* Morales.

His wife pulled a bucket of water up from the well as Miguel approached the house. "He is at the mission, Miguel."

Señor Morales was giving orders to men who were filling cracks and holes with handfuls of thick, brown mud.

"Miguel, there you are," he said. "After we paint the building with whitewash, will you make a decoration for the mission? Can you do it?"

"That is what I've been thinking about, *Señor*."

"Good, but don't take all year. Remember, the new *padre* will be here on Christmas Eve. Just a few days."

For the rest of the afternoon, Miguel leaned against a boulder, chewing a strip of sugar cane, and gazing at the mission wall. What kind of picture should he make? What was most beautiful?

He closed his eyes and imagined tiny chickens with irridescent black feathers and flowing, feathery top-knots; wet sand that glistened like undersea diamonds; he even thought of a fish, brown and crisp in the pan. Perhaps his father had caught a fish after all. But of course he could not make a picture of these for the mission. Miguel went home.

The next day Miguel burned tree twigs for charcoal, and with broad, free strokes, he sketched the outline of a baby on the wall. He would use the most interesting and beautiful of all materials—the pebbles.

He would have liked to lean against the rock and study his design for a while, but *Señor* Morales was standing just a few feet away, scowling with his arms folded across his chest. Several people of Sal Agua watched, and when Miguel told them he would make a picture of the baby Jesus, they just smiled and waited.

"Don't forget, Miguel, tonight is the first night of the *Posadas*. You have only eight days until the new *padre* comes," someone said.

The pebbles were heavy, and Miguel was out of breath when he put the basket on the ground by the mission. But he would have to make many more trips to his house.

He began cementing the pebbles in place. He chose each one carefully for its special color, shape, and texture. Now on the mission, in the center of Sal Agua, everyone could enjoy their beauty. As he worked people stopped to see what he had brought to their mission. Miguel heard

sounds of puzzlement and disappointment. It was inevitable that *Señor* Morales would appear.

"Miguel, what is this you are doing to the mission? Why have you stuck rocks on our clean church wall?"

"I have just begun to make a picture of the infant Jesus. Can't you tell? When I've finished, you will see it."

Señor Morales was not pleased.

That night Miguel and his parents joined the *Posada* procession. They walked from house to house and asked for shelter for an imaginary Joseph and Mary. It was a rule of the pageant that they would be refused entrance at every house. Only on the last night, Christmas Eve, would a door be opened. In Sal Agua, it would be the mission door.

Miguel's picture grew. Carefully he searched until he found the most delicate pink pebbles for the infant's face and hands. Often he chose a pebble thinking at first that it was right. But upon finding that it lacked the color or texture, he kept looking until he found just the right one. Each claimed a unique secret. Each had been tossed around in the sea, absorbing color and roughness and smoothness. This picture would be the most beautiful he had ever made.

But it was plain to see that the villagers did not share his belief.

"Miguel, why aren't you using the brightly colored glass which adorns your own house?"

Miguel answered, "The glass, being glass, is only clear. One can see it all. There is no mystery. In pebbles, there is mystery and more color than one can see anywhere else."

The villagers grumbled.

Señor Morales said, "The truth is that Miguel is a lazy boy. We have always known it. It is too much work for him to break up the colored glass, even for the mission."

Someone said, "Perhaps he does not want any place in the village

44

to look more beautiful than his own house. Could that be the reason?"

"It's because I want the mission to be beautiful that I am using the pebbles," Miguel replied.

Almost everyone who watched shook his head in disappointment, and some in wonder at what the *padre* would say.

"Miguel," said *Señor* Morales, "ever since you were a small boy, you could make pictures and draw things. Now when it is important, you make an ugly picture on our mission—yes, ugly. I don't know what the *padre* will say about your spoiling the wall."

Miguel was left by himself. The wind from the sea blew cold about his ears. He wrapped the *serape* tightly about his shoulders and walked home. He stretched out on his straw mat which was inches too short for his legs. His pictures were everywhere—on the walls and on the table. Even when he threw one which was not good in the fire, his mother would leap to save it. She had shown all the pictures at least once to everyone who came to visit.

He took a pebble from his pocket. "Mother, look at this. Don't you call it beautiful? It looks as though the whole earth had pressed upon a ball of grass."

His mother let it roll over in her hard, brown palm. "Miguel, my dear, the bright glass is more beautiful to me, but it has always taken me longer to see the beauty that you see at once."

He put his finger to his mouth and moistened the pebble. "It's even more mysterious looking and its color is deeper when it is wet."

Miguel joined the *Posadas* procession each night, but no one stood nearer the end of the line than he. As he sang the song asking for shelter, his throat tightened and almost trapped the song inside his body.

Few would look at the mission wall, and when they did they quickly looked up as though asking forgiveness for it. Besides his parents only young children talked to Miguel.

It was cloudy and chill. The outdoor brick ovens blazed a welcome warmth on the day before Christmas. Sweet cakes and cookies baked for the *piñata* party which would welcome the new *padre* to Sal Agua. Children shinnied up the lime trees which grew around the mission, and brought down the sweet fruit; grown-ups hiked into the hills for ripe apples and stalks of sugar cane for the *piñata*. In spite of the flurry of activity, the usual Christmas-time gaiety and merriment were missing.

Miguel cemented the last of the pebbles in his picture of the infant Jesus. Several people stopped to see it, perhaps hoping a change had occurred overnight. *Señor* Morales talked loudly against Miguel, of how he would cover the pebbles with whitewash or even knock them off if the mission wall were strong enough.

"Surely you will not be bold enough to share this last *Posadas* with us, Miguel, after what you've done. I will speak for the villagers and ask you not to come. Perhaps you have learned a lesson, Miguel."

46

A light rain fell on Sal Agua, stopping just before the villagers gathered to sing the last *Posadas*. Everyone except Miguel and his parents gathered in front of *Señor* Morales' house. There each person lit a candle.

From their window, Miguel and his parents watched as *Señor* Morales and his wife led the procession carrying small images of Joseph and Mary. Miguel could feel the tingle of excitement in the people at having their own *padre* at last. Miguel knew that in spite of their disappointment in him and the picture, they would welcome the *padre* with great happiness and relief.

At each house except Miguel's the group paused and asked for admission. When it was time to go to the mission, *Señor* Morales said importantly, "Let us hope the new *padre* has not seen the ugly picture."

Before the door of the mission they gathered as tightly as their lighted candles would allow. When they sang the plea for shelter, the mission door opened, and even Miguel from his window could see the

47

bright green and red star *piñata* which hung in the entrance hall. The *piñata* would be filled to the top with sugar cane, limes, and apples.

However, the villagers scarcely noticed the *piñata*. In the soft glow of the candlelight, the pebble picture caught their eyes. It was wet and shiny from the rain, and it shone with a beauty that transcended the light of the candles.

"It is as Miguel has said, a picture of the infant Jesus," they said, looking at one another.

Miguel and his parents saw that the *padre* also looked approvingly at the picture. Some of the people, including *Señor* Morales, went inside the mission. But many more walked toward Miguel's house.

"We should have trusted you, Miguel, the one among us who always has seen beauty where we were blind. You have worked very hard."

Miguel and his parents joined the villagers for one of the gayest Christmas Eve parties that they could remember. From then on, whenever damp, gray days made the picture vivid and beautiful, it brought cheer to all people.

And even when the pebbles were dry, the people of Sal Agua could see the beauty in Miguel's picture when they really looked.

HOW TO USE A PIÑATA

"I think I'll give a party" is usually a happy decision. It is also one which presents problems. Plans for almost any kind of party bring up the question, "How shall I decorate the room?" Decorations can add much to the atmosphere and mood of a party. But they can also cause the cost to skyrocket.

With its brilliant colors and festive appearance, the *piñata* as a decoration is a handsome, inexpensive eyecatcher. A *piñata* is an on-the-spot ice-breaker and conversation-starter. Or it can be an exciting climax to games and entertainment. Who can help wondering what delicacies are in a *piñata*? But that is only one reason for its appeal.

A *piñata* at parties can be used to replace the traditional, party-weary nut cups and favors. Most important, a *piñata* provides fun. It is an exciting game that extends a rare invitation to break something, an enormously satisfying stunt. There is suspense, surprise, and competition in both the breaking and in the scramble for gifts or treats.

A filled *piñata* is suspended by a rope at a height just above arm's reach of those who will play the game. Sometimes for very young children the *piñata* is placed on a low bench or stool, but traditionally it is hung from the ceiling—from a beam or door facing, from a balcony, or, when the party takes place outside, a tree limb. It is important that the rope by which the *piñata* is suspended be strung through a hook or over a pulley, or be otherwise movable. The contestant is blindfolded and led to a spot beneath the *piñata*. There he is given a broomstick. The *piñata* should be given a swing so that it sways back and forth, thus making the blindfolded person's task even more difficult. The contestant usually is allowed three strikes at the *piñata*. If he fails to break it, other contestants are chosen or appointed by the hostess until eventually the *piñata* is broken, and the mad scramble for treats or gifts begins.

There are a few points to keep in mind when entertaining either children or grown-ups. One is to be sure that the guests direct their smashing efforts toward the *piñata*. Frequently, the onlookers need reminders to stand out of the way of such feverish batting. This can be more easily accomplished by the establishing of a boundary line. The *piñata* area could be encircled with either a rope or a chalk line. All players must then

stand beyond the boundary until the *piñata* is demolished and the batting has ceased.

It should also be understood by all players at the beginning of the game that a command of "stop" by the leader must be obeyed at once. The blindfolded person must not wander among the other players swinging the stick.

Something which is almost as much fun as breaking the *piñata*, is filling it. You may ask guests to bring with them something which they would like to put in the *piñata*. It may be a small possession of their own with which they are ready to part, a gag gift, or a trinket purchased for the occasion. They may drop it in the *piñata* when they arrive. In any event, you as hostess would do well to specify the size limitations of the gift. The openings of a *piñata* for which instructions are given in this book are 3″ x 3″, but they can of course be made larger if you wish.

On the other hand, you may choose to furnish all the treats yourself. Probably one of the most important points to remember, if you are giving a party for a very young person, is to retain behind the scene a generous reserve of the same treats with which you have stuffed the *piñata*. Invariably, a timid guest or a late-starter will emerge from the

fray clutching a lone piece of bubble gum, while the more aggressive ones will have finished by filling every available pocket. Treats held in reserve for such emergencies will help stave off disappointment.

Piñatas may be bought in many department stores and ordered through some mail-order houses, but creating a *piñata* is a happy experience.

Each year many clubs mull over an assortment of ideas, searching for ways in which their groups can earn money. Your club may look with favor on a *piñata* making-and-selling project.

It has been demonstrated many times that a *piñata*-making project can be, unlike the ordinary fund raising project, a very happy occasion.

If you prefer an assembly line technique, the materials should be purchased ahead of time (See *How to Make a Piñata*). Making the *piñata* can be divided roughly into tasks for three groups: the balloon inflators and paper strip appliers, the decoration cutters, and the decorators. The group assigned the first task should finish its work a day or two in advance of the time set for completing the *piñatas*. This assembly line method is fastest, but, as in other such productions, the finished product doesn't reflect individual creativity.

The method which is the most fun is the one in which each member

makes his own *piñata* from start to finish, pretty or funny as he chooses.

Once the *piñatas* are completed, the group may choose to sell them either empty or filled with treats; or may give them to institutions—children's homes, hospitals, or orphanages. A check may be included among the treats. Be sure to include also directions for playing the *piñata* game.

A young people's church group may think of the *piñata* as a way of spreading good cheer during the holidays. The *piñata* may be filled with small toys for children of a needy family, or money for the family, or with both.

Club members who are responsible for decorating a banquet room may use the *piñata*. The basic form can then be less sturdy, and of course, the fewer layers of paper strips, the shorter the drying time (See *How to Make a Piñata*). One *piñata* can be made in several color combinations, or several *piñatas* can be made in identical color schemes.

Miniature *piñatas* add charm to any occasion and require less work to make.

Because of the almost unlimited range of color, shape, and contents which may be used, the *piñata* idea can be used again and again and still retain its freshness.

Although the party you are planning may not fit precisely into one of the following categories, the ideas may be helpful to you. You may wish to plan a party for yourself and your friends, a younger brother or sister, or even for a grown-up.

New Year's Eve

Use the Star *piñata*. Fill with noisemakers and confetti.

Valentine's Day

Use the Cake *piñata*. Decorate in red and white and fill with red hots, candy hearts, and valentines.

Easter

Use the Easter Egg *piñata*. Fill with wrapped marshmallow bunnies, candy Easter eggs, yellow cotton baby chicks, pastel confetti.

Fourth of July

Use the Drum *piñata*. Fill with candy mints, whistles, small plastic army men and tanks, red, white, and blue candies.

Halloween

Use Witch or Jack O'Lantern *piñata*. Fill with licorice candies, orange gumdrops, black half-masks, and small packs of stage makeup such as putty blacking and white greasepaint.

Christmas

Use the Santa Claus or Star *piñata*. This is an ideal time to invite guests to exchange small gifts. Fill the *piñata* with gifts and with miniature filled Christmas stockings.

After-the-Game Party

Use the Football or the Star *piñata*. Make it in the team colors and fill with foil-wrapped candy kisses and perhaps one or two tickets to the next game.

Going-Away or Welcome-Back Party

Use the Star *piñata*. Fill with small gifts or gag gifts, and small candies or tiny bags of nuts.

Graduation Party

Use the Drum or Star *piñata*. Decorate in black and white and fill with miniature diplomas, gag gifts, and candies and nuts.

Boy's Birthday Party

Use the Drum, Donkey, Satellite, Football, or Clown *piñata*. Fill with skull rings, toy cars, trucks, cowboys, Indians, balloons, baseball or football cards, rubber lizards, snakes, airplane gliders, small sacks of marbles, paper money, rubber balls, or other small gifts. Treats may be almost any selection of nuts, candy, or fruit.

Girl's Birthday Party

Use the Star, Cake, or Clown *piñata*. Fill with miniature plastic dolls, doll baby bottles, barettes, ribbons, doll shoes, crayons, puzzles, jump ropes, dime store jewelry, and other small gifts. Treats may be any selection of nuts, candy, or fruit.

Treasure Hunt

To get a treasure hunt off to a good start, use any *piñata* appropriate to the season or the occasion. Fill it with the wrapped treats but include also slips of paper on which the clues for the treasure hunt are printed.

HOW TO MAKE A PIÑATA

If there were no way of creating a *piñata* except by making and firing a clay jar, few of us would ever know the fun of making one. Fortunately, there are other methods of making the basic form. Some are built over hatboxes. Plain paper bags can be decorated with crayon drawings. Chicken wire can be shaped and covered with cloth strips which have been dipped in plaster of paris. One of the best ways to make a *piñata* is to cover a balloon.

Most of the *piñatas* in this book begin with balloons. The balloon may be round, egg shaped, long, or a combination of these shapes.

All of the basic balloon forms are covered by the application of several layers of paper strips which have been dipped in liquid laundry starch or a flour and water paste.

Many *piñatas* are very simple to make. Others require more attention to details and measurements, but none are really difficult if the directions are followed carefully.

MATERIALS NEEDED FOR PIÑATAS

The following list will give you an idea of the materials you can use in making *piñatas*. You will not need all of them for any one *piñata*.

newspapers

liquid laundry starch

flour and water paste (one part flour to two parts water)

rubber cement

tissue paper, 20″ x 30″ (this can be found at stationery and art supply stores)

crepe paper, 20″ x 7½′

construction paper, 12″ x 18″ (unless otherwise specified in directions for a given *piñata*)

small paintbrush

hemp rope or sturdy mailing twine

scissors

yardstick

pencil, chalk, or crayon

balloons

Read the directions for making a specific model before gathering your materials.

Assemble all the materials needed for the *piñata* of your choice. Inflate the balloon or balloons to the specified size. Knot or secure with thread so that the air does not escape. If two or more balloons are to be joined (as in the Clown or Santa Claus *piñata*) spread rubber cement over a three inch square area of each stem end. Press the balloons together gently for a few minutes until a firm grip has been established.

Joining two balloons for Clown or Santa Claus or other two-part *piñata*

NEWSPAPER STRIPS

Tear newspapers into strips 2″ wide. Lengths of the strips will need to vary so that they are long enough to go around the balloon. When two balloons are being used some of the strips must be long enough to extend lengthwise from one balloon to another for added support. Tear the newspapers rather than cut them. Tearing is much faster than cutting, and, more important, the torn edges will help to strengthen the *piñata*

59

form. Four layers of paper strips usually are sufficient to cover the balloon form. A *piñata* should not be too easy to break. On the other hand, it must not be indestructible.

APPLYING NEWSPAPER STRIPS
TO BALLOON FORM

Dip paper strips in starch or paste, wipe off excess, and apply strip around the balloon, placing the first strip just below the area to be allowed for an opening. When more than one balloon is used, secure the two together by extending paper strips up and down from one balloon to the other. This is necessary to give the *piñata* uniform strength. It is important to remember this step if the head of the *piñata* is not to be severed from the body at the first blow of the stick.

Since wet newspaper strips are an indistinguishable mass, it is difficult to remember how many layers of paper strips have been applied to a balloon. The easiest way to assist the memory is to alternate with each layer of paper strips the direction in which the strips are applied. Again, four layers of strips usually are enough to give uniform strength to the *piñata* form.

A paste-covered balloon is an unbelievably slippery object on which to keep even a mildly firm grip. A dish towel placed under the balloon will keep it immobilized until the first layer of paper strips has been applied. After the first layer is on, the *piñata* form is less apt to skid about.

Where *piñatas* are to have arms and legs, these should usually be applied after the last layer of newspaper strips and paste. They stick much more firmly while the form is still wet.

Applying paper strips which
have been dipped in starch
or paste

DRAWING GUIDE LINES ON THE
PIÑATA

To assist in the decoration of the *piñata* it may be desirable to have certain guide lines. Such lines will vary with the shapes of the *piñatas*, but after the form is dry the lines can be drawn with chalk or crayon.

The purpose of the lines is to dissect the *piñata* into easily identifiable parts.

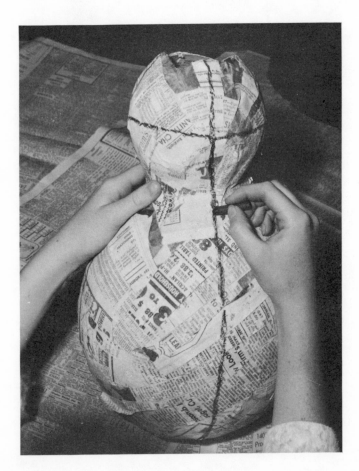

Making guide lines on *piñata*

ATTACHING A HARNESS TO
THE PIÑATA FORM

When the form is thoroughly dried, deflate the balloon by sticking a pin in it. Nearly always the balloon will then shrivel and fall to the bottom of the form. If any part of the balloon remains at the *piñata* opening, cut it away.

The form now must be outfitted with a harness of light hemp rope

Securing rope harness with paper stickers. Masking tape can be used if preferred.

or twine with which to suspend it. Attach the harness so that it encircles the *piñata* from bottom to top. Masking tape or other sturdy gummed tape will be helpful in attaching the rope. Make a stout loop at the top. To this loop the remaining part of the rope will be tied after the decoration is completed, in order to suspend the *piñata*.

Making hole for rope harness for certain *piñatas*

DECORATING THE *PIÑATA*

Cutting Tissue Paper Ruffles

   With the sheet of tissue paper folded crosswise, measure and cut strips three inches wide. Each strip will be 3″ x 30″. Fold each strip in half lengthwise. Fringe the strip by cutting from the *folded* edge to within ½″ of the cut side. These slashes should be approximately ⅛″ apart. Many ruffles can be made at one time by folding four or five strips of paper together.

Cutting paper ruffling

Turning and Refolding the Tissue Ruffle

Newspapers should be spread on your work area to absorb the excess color from dampened tissue or crepe paper. Unfold the paper ruffle with folded side up, and use a small paintbrush to spread liquid starch or commercial paste on one edge of the ruffle. Small dabs at two- or three-inch intervals will do the job. Refold the strip in the reverse direction from which it was originally folded. By making a few ruffles you will learn just how much paste or adhesive is necessary to form a bond without causing the tissue to tear. While flour-and-water paste has adhesive qualities, it is notorious for leaving white, powdery smudges on colored paper. Use rubber cement where its use is suggested. Unlike water-base adhesives it does the job without causing colors to run and tissue paper to crinkle. It cements cleanly without leaving a pasty residue.

Reversing and pasting paper ruffling

Attaching ruffling
to *piñata*

Applying the Tissue Ruffle

With the brush, apply starch or paste to the *piñata* form on a small area at a time. Lay ruffling over *piñata* form in direction specified. Each row of ruffling should be applied to the form in such a way that only the actual ruffle of the preceding row is visible.

When the ruffling is being applied, place the *piñata* form in a mixing bowl just a trifle larger than the form. It will not only confine it to a small area but will help prevent unnecessary crushing of the completed

67

piñata. Or the form may be suspended from a doorway or light fixture while you are decorating it.

For a more attractive *piñata* the ruffling can be extended over the area allowed for the *piñata* opening, but be sure to leave the rope loop exposed. When the *piñata* is ready for filling, a small slit is made through the tissue paper around three edges of the area originally allowed for the opening. The flap then can be discreetly replaced and you may safely challenge anyone to pinpoint the exact location of the opening.

INSERTING GIFTS OR TREATS
IN THE *PIÑATA*

In planning your *piñata* you must allow an area for the opening. The size of the opening in which the gifts or treats are inserted will depend on the size and quantity of the treats.

If you are using the usual wrapped candies, gum, and nuts, plan for a 3″ x 3″ opening at the top or upper side of the *piñata* where it does not interfere with the loop of rope or twine from which the *piñata* is to be suspended (See *Attaching a Harness to the Piñata Form*).

On an average the treat-holding capacity of the *piñatas* described in this book will be for about twenty-five guests if the treats are to be candies and nuts. If larger gifts are used, the opening will need to be appropriately larger than the 3″ x 3″ suggested here, and the *piñata* will serve fewer guests. Of course it is always possible to make a larger *piñata*.

TO SUSPEND A *PIÑATA*

In order to suspend the *piñata* tie one end of a length of clothesline rope or other sturdy rope to the end of the *piñata* harness.

A yard, patio, or large play room usually is a practical location for breaking a *piñata* since the activity requires ample "swinging room." For older players it is important that the *piñata* be maneuvered up and down so that it evades the swinging bat or stick of the blindfolded contestant. This movability may be achieved by tossing the free end of rope over a sturdy tree limb or through a large hook from the beam of a ceiling or from the top of a door facing.

For young children, the *piñata* may simply be tied to the top of a stool. Hitting a stationary object while blindfolded usually is challenge enough for young children, especially if the contestant himself is turned around two or three times after being blindfolded.

ONE MORE THING

Now that the *piñata* is completed, will you almost hate to see it broken? Why not make it a couple of weeks in advance of the time you plan to use it? Hang it in an appropriate place as a decoration. As time goes by it may become less dear and you may even look forward to the fun of breaking it.

The colors used in the instructions which follow are merely examples of the almost unlimited combinations which can be used. Do not be concerned if there are variations between the *piñatas* you make and the ones described in this book. Yours will be just as attractive and probably just what you wanted in the first place. The patterns could be easily adapted for other *piñatas*.

Let your imagination soar. Remember—with a *piñata* almost anything goes. The brighter, the gayer, the wilder, the better!

BIRTHDAY CAKE

You will need:

    1 ladies' hatbox, round, 8″ high and 16″ in diameter
    6 sheets of colored tissue paper, 20″ x 30″
    jumbo drinking straws, for candles
    starch or paste
    12 feet of hemp rope, for the harness and to suspend the *piñata*

Cut opening in lid of box, 3″ x 3″. Paste lid to box and tie rope harness on hatbox as though you were tying for mailing. Cover entire hatbox with paper ruffling.

For candles, make two ¼″ slashes at one end of each straw. Bend the slashed portions out from the straw. Apply paste and affix to the *piñata* among the paper ruffling.

Approximate size: 10″ high x 18″ in diameter.

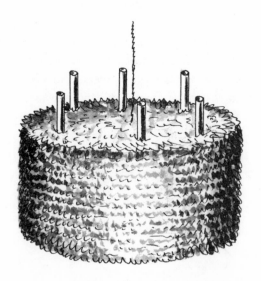

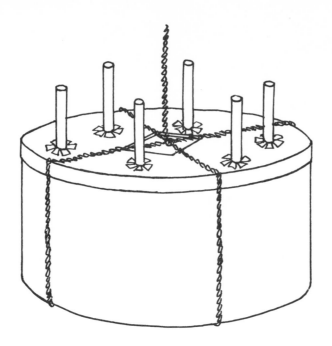

Birthday Cake *piñata* form showing rope harness

Note: If the hatbox cake seems unlikely to break, remember that with a good strong strike it will, when suspended, turn over to the extent that the gifts and treats cascade to the floor through the opening. When placed on a bench or stool for young children, the *piñata* may be mounted in such a way that it will turn over when struck to release the gifts.

CLOWN

You will need:

1 round shaped balloon that can be inflated to 11"
1 round shaped balloon that can be inflated to 5"
newspaper strips
starch or paste
10 feet of hemp rope
rubber cement
2 sheets of vivid blue tissue paper
1 sheet of matching blue construction paper, 12" x 18", for arm and leg cones
2 sheets of chartreuse tissue paper
1 sheet of matching chartreuse construction paper, 12" x 18", for arm and leg cones. If matching paper cannot be found, tissue paper may be cemented over off-white construction paper.
⅛ sheet of bright pink tissue paper, 20" x 30", for bow tie
1 sheet of white tissue paper for face and head
1 piece of gold paper or aluminum foil, 6" x 12", for hat
scrap of red construction paper, for nose and mouth
scrap of black construction paper, for eyelashes and buttons
masking tape

72

Inflate large balloon to 11″ and small one to 5″. Cement together at stem ends with rubber cement around 3″ area, and press together gently until bond is formed. Apply four layers of newspaper strips which have been dipped in starch. Leave uncovered area at top of small balloon, 3″ x 3″, for *piñata* opening. Allow to dry, then deflate balloons. Draw continuous line from top of head down center front, over and under body and up back to top of head. Draw another line down each side of the *piñata* form, beginning at top of head. Draw a horizontal line around head, halfway between top of head and neck. Attach harness as shown in photograph (page 63) by punching two small holes in *piñata* where head joins body. Put one hole on each side. Affix the rope to the body with masking tape, inserting each end of the rope through one of the holes on the side and pulling the ends out the open space at the top. Be sure to make a loop for tying to the suspension cord.

Cut a circle, 8″ in diameter, of vivid blue construction paper. Cut a circle, 8″ in diameter, of chartreuse construction paper. Cut each circle in half and fold each of four pieces into a cone shape. Cement straight edges of each cone together. Make ⅜″ cuts around bottom edges of four cones and bend edges outward. With rubber cement, attach one cone of each color on each side of Clown's body, on side lines two inches down from neck to form arms. Attach remaining two cones, with color matching upper cones, on side lines, 1½″ from bottom center of clown to form legs.

Cover head with white tissue paper ruffling. Using center and back guide lines, cover one side of clown with blue ruffling and the other side with chartreuse ruffling. Cut eyelashes from black and cut nose and mouth from red construction paper. Attach nose in front center of head. Cement eyelashes 1½″ from each side of nose, so that lower edge of lashes is on a level with top of nose. Cement mouth 1″ below nose.

Cut bow of pink tissue paper, 20″ x 3″. Fold crosswise in thirds.

Gather bow in the center and secure with string or gummed tape. Cement bow tie on *piñata* at front base of head, or just below mouth. Cut 3 buttons 1½″ in diameter from black construction paper. Cement buttons down center front at 1½″ intervals. Cement straight edges of hat. Tassels may be made, if desired. See pattern on page 76. Insert tassel before cementing edges of hat. Cement to head of clown with rubber cement. By positioning hat on form before cementing, it can be placed beside the rope, so that the loop is left exposed for attaching to suspension rope. Be sure to leave rope loop exposed. Attach remainder of rope to loop.

Approximate size: 20″ high.

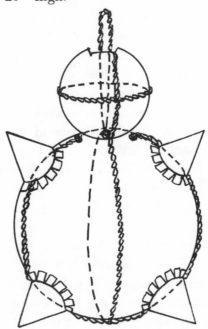

Clown *piñata* form showing guide lines, rope harness, and placement of arms and legs

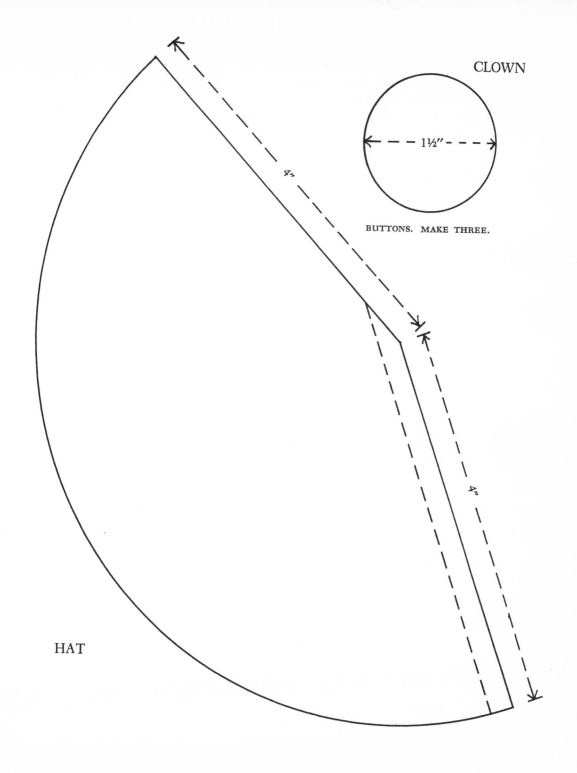

CLOWN

1½″

BUTTONS. MAKE THREE.

4"

4"

HAT

CLOWN

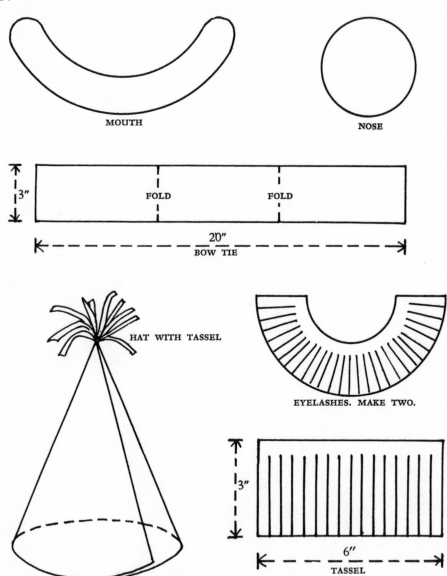

MOUTH

NOSE

3″

FOLD   FOLD

20″
BOW TIE

HAT WITH TASSEL

EYELASHES. MAKE TWO.

3″

6″
TASSEL

DONKEY

You will need:

     1 round shaped balloon that can be inflated to 11″
     newspaper strips
     starch or paste
     newspapers
     aluminum foil, 6″ x 12″
     5 sheets of green tissue paper, 20″ x 30″
     2 sheets of yellow tissue paper, 20″ x 30″
     black construction paper, 8″ x 2½″
     10 feet of hemp rope
     rubber cement or commercial paste
     stapler

Inflate balloon to 11″ and tie. Apply four layers of newspaper strips which have been dipped in starch or paste, leaving 3″ x 3″ area uncovered

for *piñata* opening. While Donkey *piñata* is wet with paste, attach legs, neck, and tail.

Cut neck and head from four thicknesses of newspapers, 12″ x 11″. Form into a roll 4 or 5″ in diameter and 11″ long, and staple at overlapping seam ends to secure. Make a fold 7″ from one end to form the head. Fill head end with crumpled newspaper. Other end becomes the neck. Make 1″ cuts at end of neck and attach to Donkey's body as shown in diagram. For legs cut four 10″ circles from four thicknesses of newspaper. Cut circles in half and staple together, for ease in handling, the four sheets in each half circle. Each half circle will be composed of four sheets of newspaper stapled together. Form a cone from each of the half circles, and cement or paste the straight edges together. Make 1″ cuts along bottom (open end) of the cones, apply paste or rubber cement, and attach to *piñata* form as shown in diagram.

Make tail by forming a roll, 1½″ in diameter and 9″ long of several thicknesses of newspaper. Secure roll with glue or gummed tape, or by stapling. Make 1″ cuts at one end of the roll; fold back the cut portions, apply paste or rubber cement, and attach to Donkey *piñata* as shown in diagram.

Allow *piñata* form to dry. Deflate balloon and tie rope harness around middle of *piñata* form.

Make ruffling of aluminum foil and apply two rows around tip of each leg. Cover body and legs of Donkey with green tissue ruffling. Using pattern, make ears of black construction paper and ear lining of aluminum foil. Paste ear lining in center of ears and make a slight lengthwise crease down the middle of each one. Staple or glue to sides of head at fold (between head and neck).

Cover neck and head of Donkey with yellow tissue ruffling, extending over nose end of head. Cut eyes of white paper and draw black circles in

78

them with pencil or ink. Glue on top of head about 2″ from nose end.
Cut mouth of red construction paper, using pattern, and glue on front
of nose. Tail may be covered with either green or aluminum foil ruffling.
Attach remaining rope to existing loop.

Approximate size: 20″ long.

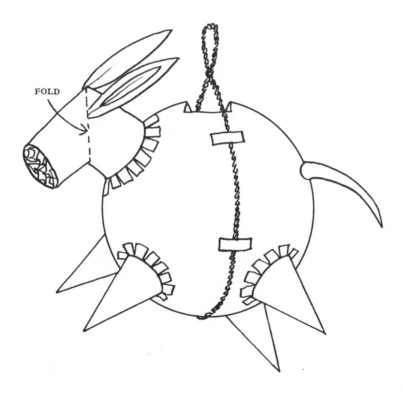

Donkey *piñata* form showing harness, positioning of legs,
neck, and tail

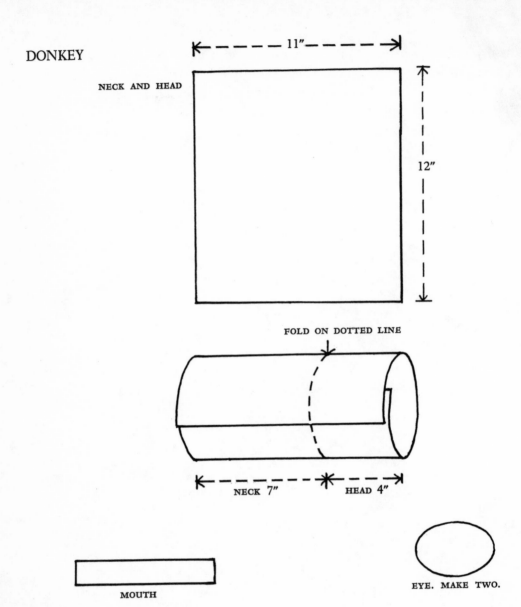

DONKEY

NECK AND HEAD

11"

12"

FOLD ON DOTTED LINE

NECK 7"   HEAD 4"

MOUTH

EYE. MAKE TWO.

DONKEY

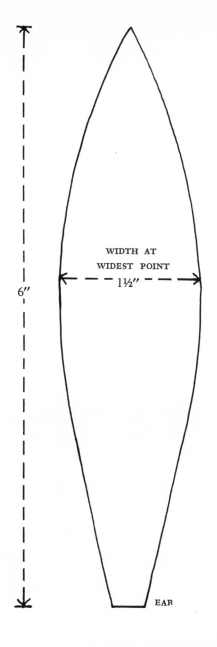

WIDTH AT
WIDEST POINT
1½″

6″

EAR

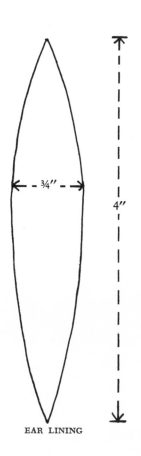

¾″

4″

EAR LINING

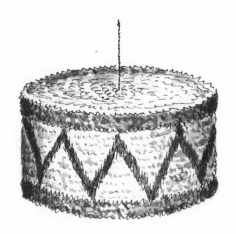

DRUM

You will need:

    1 ladies' hatbox, round, about 8″ high and 16″ in diameter

    3 sheets of white tissue paper, 20″ x 30″

    2 sheets of red tissue paper, 20″ x 30″

    1 sheet of blue tissue paper, 20″ x 30″

    12 feet of light hemp rope. A part of the rope will be used to harness the *piñata*. The balance will be used for suspension rope.

Cut opening in lid of box 3″ x 3″. Paste lid to box and tie rope harness on hatbox as though tying a package for mailing. Make secure loop at top for tying to suspension rope.

Draw a line around the drum 1½″ down from top edge. Draw a second line around the drum 1½″ from bottom edge of drum. Draw a continuous diagonal line connecting top and bottom lines.

Cover top and bottom of drum with white tissue ruffling. With red tissue ruffling cover 1½" at top and bottom as indicated by lines mentioned above (to be drawn around the drum). Cover continuous diagonal line with blue tissue ruffling. Fill in areas between diagonal blue lines with white tissue ruffling.

Attach suspension rope to loop. Approximate size: 10" high and 18" in diameter

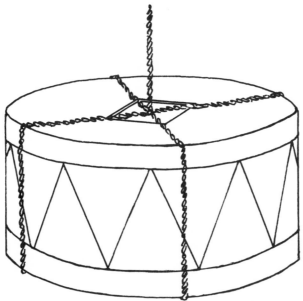

Drum with guide lines for decorating and showing position of rope harness

Note: If the hatbox drum seems unlikely to break, remember that with a good strong strike it will, when suspended, turn over to the extent that the gifts and treats cascade to the floor through the opening. When placed on a bench for young children the *piñata* may be mounted in such a way that it turns over when struck to release the gifts.

EASTER EGG

You will need:
    1 egg-shaped balloon that can be inflated to 15″ in length
    newspaper strips
    starch or paste
    rubber cement
    10 feet of hemp rope
    1 sheet of lavender tissue paper, 20″ x 30″
    ¼ sheet of purple tissue paper, 20″ x 30″
    2 sheets of light pink tissue paper, 20″ x 30″
    1 sheet of dark pink tissue paper, 20″ x 30″
    1 sheet of yellow construction paper, 3″ x 12″

Inflate balloon to a length of 15″ and tie. Apply four layers of newspaper strips which have been dipped in starch or paste. Leave an uncovered area, 3″ x 3″ on the side of the balloon for *piñata* opening. Allow to dry and deflate balloon. Attach rope harness as shown in diagram.

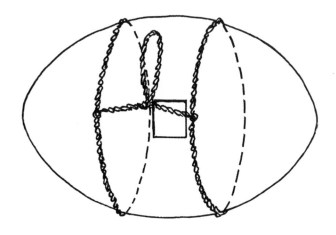

Easter Egg *piñata* form showing rope harness

To decorate, apply ten or eleven rows of light pink tissue ruffling, beginning at one end. Apply one row of dark pink ruffling, six rows of lavendar ruffling, one row of dark pink, then eight rows of light pink ruffling. Complete by pasting two more rows of dark pink ruffling, then with sufficient rows of light pink ruffling to finish *piñata*.

Cut four circles of purple tissue paper, 1½″ in diameter. Cut four circles 1½″ in diameter, of yellow construction paper.

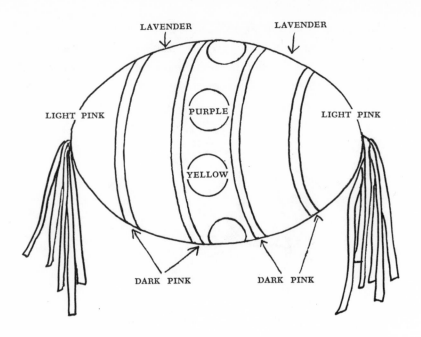

Easter Egg *piñata* showing guide lines for divisions of color and placement of circles

Alternating colors, attach the circles with rubber cement around center light pink section. Streamers are optional, but they may be made by cutting six strips of tissue paper, 13″ x 3″. Use colors which have been used for the egg. Cut each strip lengthwise to within ½″ of end, making ¼″ cuts so the streamers will be in ¼″ widths. With rubber cement, attach half of the strips to one end of *piñata*, and half to the other end. Ends may be curled by twirling gently over scissors. Complete the *piñata* by attaching remainder of rope to the existing loop.

Approximate size: 17″ in length.

86

FOOTBALL

You will need:

    1 egg-shaped balloon that can be inflated to 15″ in length

    newspaper strips

    starch or paste

    6 feet of hemp rope

    rubber cement

    3 sheets of brown tissue paper, 20″ x 30″

    1 sheet of white tissue paper, 20″ x 30″

    4″ square of white cardboard or construction paper

Inflate balloon to a length of 15″ and tie. Following directions given in first part of chapter, apply four layers of newspaper strips which have been dipped in starch. Leave a 3″ x 3″ uncovered area in center of balloon for opening. (Instructions continue on next page.)

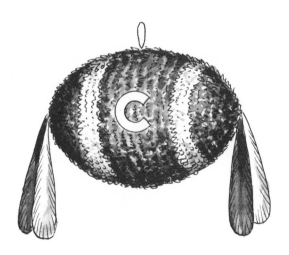

Allow to dry and deflate balloon. Attach rope harness as shown in diagram for Easter Egg *piñata*.

Beginning at one end of *piñata* form, apply ten or eleven rows of brown tissue ruffling. Next apply two rows of white ruffling, then eight rows of brown, two rows of white, and complete with brown tissue ruffling.

Cut from white cardboard or paper a monogram of your family, town, or school team and attach with rubber cement in center of middle brown section. The monogram should be visible when the *piñata* is in a hanging position. A monogram may be placed on every side.

Cut two strips of white tissue paper and two strips of brown paper, each 13" x 3". Round off corners at end of each strip. Make ½" diagonal cuts, ¼" apart up sides of paper strips. Attach strips of both colors to each end of football *piñata*.

Approximate size: 17 inches long.

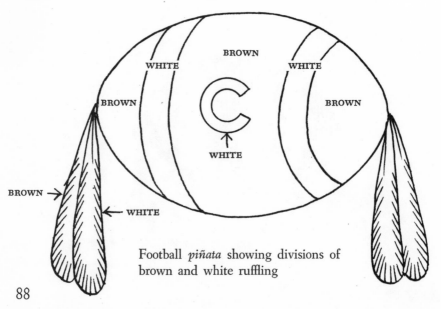

Football *piñata* showing divisions of brown and white ruffling

JACK-O'-LANTERN

You will need:

    1 round balloon that can be inflated to 11″

    newspaper strips

    starch or paste

    10 feet of light hemp rope

    3 sheets of orange tissue paper, 20″ x 30″

    ¼ sheet of green tissue paper, 20″ x 30″

    1 sheet of black construction paper, 9″ x 12″

    masking tape

    rubber cement

    1 sheet of white construction paper, 9″ x 12″

Inflate balloon to 11″ and tie. Apply four layers of newspaper strips which have been dipped in starch. Leave *piñata* opening, 3″ x 3″ about

2 inches down from stem end. Encircle stem end with newspaper strips, about 3" x 3", so that the stem stands upright. It will become the green stem of the pumpkin or Jack-O'-Lantern. Allow *piñata* form to dry and deflate balloon. With rope tie harness as shown in diagram. Use masking tape or other gummed tape to secure the harness if necessary. Be sure to leave a sturdy loop when tying harness so that the remainder of the rope may be attached at the appropriate time.

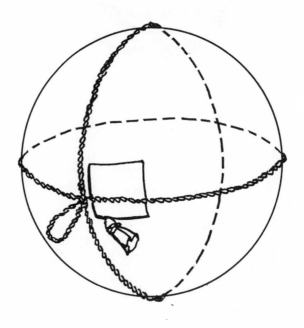

Jack-O'-Lantern form showing harness and *piñata* opening

Cover stem end with green ruffles. Cover body of Jack-O'-Lantern with orange tissue ruffles. Using patterns in diagram, cut facial features. You will need two each of Eyes "A" and "B." Eyes "B" and Mouth "B" are to be cut from white construction paper. All other features are cut from black construction paper. Cut out the dotted portion of Eye "A" and paste or cement over Eye "B." Cement Mouth "A" over Mouth "B." You will have discovered that the eyes and mouth marked "B" are white to give the impression of the whites of the eyes and of teeth. Cement the black nose in front center of the *piñata*. Cement eyes 1½" on either side of nose with lower edge of eye on level with top point of nose. Cement mouth 2" below nose. Complete the *piñata* by attaching remainder of rope to the loop.

Approximate size: 13" in diameter

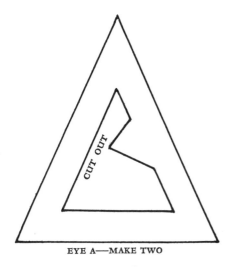

EYE A—MAKE TWO

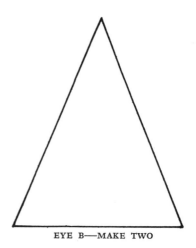

EYE B—MAKE TWO

Diagrams continued on next page.

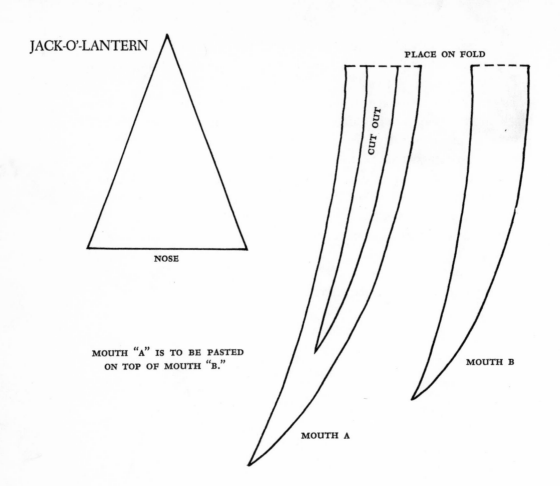

JACK-O'-LANTERN

NOSE

PLACE ON FOLD

CUT OUT

MOUTH "A" IS TO BE PASTED
ON TOP OF MOUTH "B."

MOUTH A

MOUTH B

SANTA CLAUS

This Santa Claus *piñata* was designed by Mrs. Peggy Aubrey Hulse, Claremont, California, and is used here with her permission.

You will need:
> 1 round balloon that can be inflated to 11"
> 1 round balloon that can be inflated to 5"
> newspaper strips
> starch or paste
> rubber cement
> 10 feet of hemp rope
> 1 small Christmas ball, tree ornament type
> 3 sheets of red tissue paper, 20" x 30"
> 1½ sheets of white tissue paper, 20" 30"
> ¼ sheet of pink tissue paper, 20" x 30"
> ½ sheet of black tissue paper, 20" x 30"
> 1 sheet of red construction paper, 18" x 24"
> 1 sheet of black construction paper, 12" x 18"
> 1 piece of gold paper or aluminum foil, 2½" x 2½"
> masking tape

Inflate large balloon to 11" and small one to 5"; tie. Apply cement around 3" area at stem ends and press together gently for a few minutes. Apply four layers of newspaper strips which have been dipped in starch or paste. Leave 3" x 3" square *piñata* opening at top of small balloon. Allow form to dry and deflate balloons. Draw guide lines on *piñata* form as shown in photograph (page 62). Attach harness to Santa as shown in photograph (page 63) by punching two small holes, one on each side where head joins body. Affix the rope to the body with masking tape, inserting each end of the rope through one of the holes on the side, pulling both ends out the open space at the top. Make loop for suspension cord.

Arms and legs: Cut two circles, 8" in diameter, from red construction paper. Cut each circle in half. Fold each piece to form a cone and secure straight edges with rubber cement. Make ⅜" cuts around bottom (open end) of the four cones and bend edges outward. Spread edges with rubber cement. For arms, attach one cone on each side of body 2 inches down from neck. Use guide lines previously drawn for positioning. For legs, attach remaining two cones on side lines one and one half inches from bottom center.

Face and beard: Following pattern in diagram, cut face and beard from white construction paper. Apply horizontal rows of pink tissue ruffling from top of face down to indentation in beard. Cover lower portion of beard with white tissue ruffling.

Cut eyebrows from black construction paper as shown in diagram. Cement them, one on each side, ¾" from center of face. Cut nose from red construction paper, as shown in diagram, or use a Christmas tree ball. Cement nose in center of face approximately 1" down from eyebrows. Cut mouth from red construction paper and cement near bottom center of pink ruffling. The mustache may be cut from white tissue or bond paper. The two pieces should be cemented beneath the nose, so that the two ends of the mustache extend out beyond the sides of the nose.

94

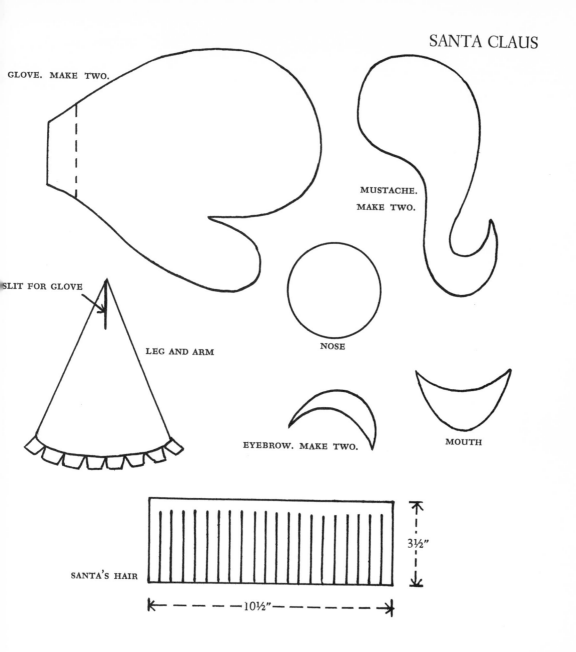

SANTA CLAUS

GLOVE. MAKE TWO.

MUSTACHE. MAKE TWO.

SLIT FOR GLOVE

LEG AND ARM

NOSE

EYEBROW. MAKE TWO.

MOUTH

SANTA'S HAIR

3½"

10½"

SANTA CLAUS

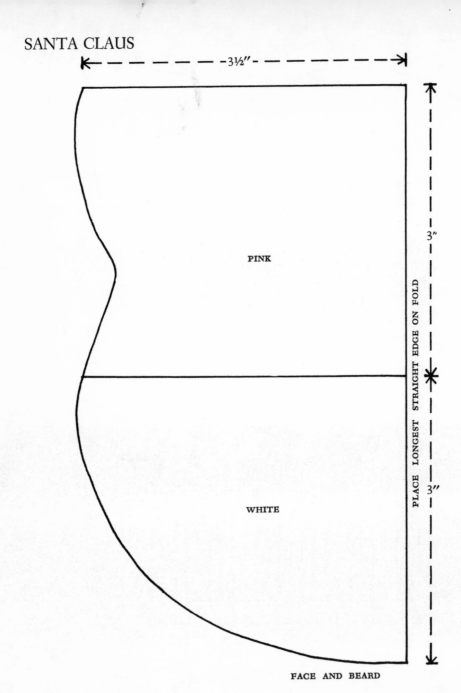

3½″

PINK

WHITE

PLACE LONGEST STRAIGHT EDGE ON FOLD

3″

3″

FACE AND BEARD

Hair: To make hair, cut from white construction paper a strip 3½" x 10½". Cover this strip with white tissue ruffling in a vertical direction. Apply rubber cement to the edge of the plain (uncovered) side of the hairpiece, and, beginning at center back guide line, bring hair around so that one side of the hairpiece meets each side of the face and beard. Apply rows of white ruffling around the crown of the head, beginning at the top of the hairpiece in back and at the top of the face in front. Cover *piñata* opening with ruffling.

Covering arms and legs: Beginning at tips of arm cones, cover with red tissue ruffling. Beginning at tips of legs, apply four rows of black tissue ruffling. Complete legs with red ruffling.

Cover remainder of Santa *piñata* with red ruffling.

Belt: For belt cut a strip 2½" x 34" from black construction paper, and with paste or rubber cement place it around the middle of Santa's body about an inch down from his arms. Edges will not lie close to his body since the form is round but the surrounding tissue ruffling will conceal edges.

Buckle: To make buckle cut a 2½" square from gold or silver paper. Cut a 1" square from black construction paper. Paste the 1" black square on the gold square, and cement the buckle to belt in center of Santa's body.

Gloves: Cut gloves from black construction paper using pattern in diagram. With knife or scissors make a ½" slit in tip of arm cones and insert gloves. Secure with rubber cement or gummed tape.

Hat: Cut hat from red construction paper, using pattern for clown's cap on page 75. Make tassel of white tissue paper. Insert ends of tassel in hat and attach with rubber cement. Cement straight edges of hat together and place on Santa's head at a rakish angle. Remember to leave harness loop exposed so that suspension rope may be tied to it.

Approximate size: 18" high and 14" wide.

SATELLITE

You will need:

    1 round balloon that can be inflated to 11″
    3 pieces of wooden doweling, ¼″ x 26″, for antennae
    newspaper strips
    starch or paste
    rubber cement or glue
    10 feet of hemp rope
    4 sheets of dark gray tissue paper, 20″ x 30″
    ½ sheet of bright pink tissue paper, 20″ x 30″
    ⅛ sheet of yellow tissue paper, 20″ x 30″
    1 sheet of yellow construction paper, 12″ x 18″
    masking tape

Inflate balloon to 11″ and tie. Apply four layers of newspaper strips which have been dipped in starch or paste. Leave 3″ x 3″ area uncovered near stem end. Allow form to dry and deflate balloon. Attach harness as shown for Jack-O'-Lantern *piñata*.

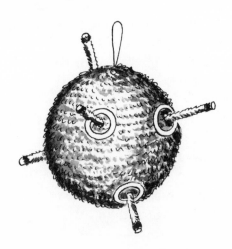

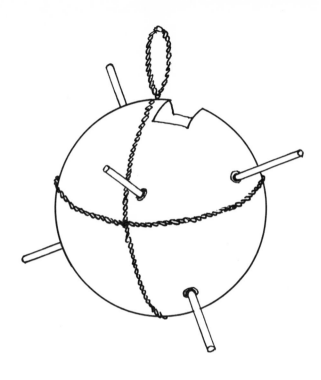

Satellite form showing position of doweling "antennae," harness, and *piñata* opening

With scissors make a small hole at the top and another at the bottom of the form. Insert one piece of doweling so that equal lengths are exposed at each end. Following the same procedure, make one small hole in each center side of *piñata* and insert one piece of doweling so that equal lengths of the doweling are exposed. Insert a third piece of doweling in holes made in front and back centers. There will be six antennae (pieces of doweling) protruding from the Satellite. Reinforce by gluing a strip of

99

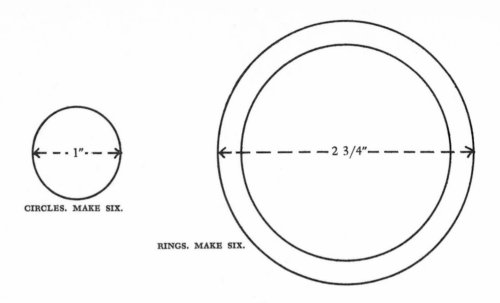

CIRCLES. MAKE SIX.

RINGS. MAKE SIX.

paper around the base of each piece of doweling where it emerges from the form.

Beginning at tip ends of doweling, attach two rows of yellow ruffling and cover remainder of doweling with pink ruffling. Cover Satellite *piñata* form with grey tissue ruffling. For Satellite rings, cut six circles 2¾″ in diameter from yellow construction paper. Trim out the inside portion of the circle so that a flat circle, ½″ wide, remains. Spread surface of circles with rubber cement or glue and attach to *piñata* at base of dowel sticks. From yellow construction paper cut six circles 1″ in diameter. Cement one circle against the tip end of each dowel stick.

Complete *piñata* by attaching remainder of rope to harness loop.

Approximate size: 27″ from one end of an antenna tip to the other end.

100

STAR

You will need:

    1 round balloon that can be inflated to 11″
    newspaper strips
    liquid starch or paste
    10 feet of hemp rope
    4 sheets of white tissue paper, 20″ x 30″
    3 sheets of blue tissue paper, 20″ x 30″
    1 sheet of magenta tissue paper, 20″ x 30″
    1 sheet of aluminum foil, 12″ x 12″
    newspapers
    masking tape
    rubber cement

Inflate balloon to 11″ and tie. Apply four layers of newspaper strips which have been dipped in starch or paste. Leave 3 x 3″ uncovered area near stem end for *piñata* opening.

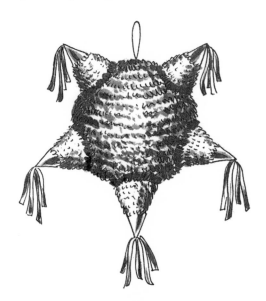

101

To make cones for five points of Star, follow the pattern shown in diagram. From three thicknesses of newspaper cut five cones, each measuring 7″ on straight sides as shown. For ease in handling individual cones it will be well, after cutting, to staple together the three flat thicknesses of newspaper in every cone. Do not form cone shapes yet. Following pattern for cone tip, cut five tips of aluminum foil, each measuring 3″ on straight sides as shown. Spread rubber cement on one side of every tip.

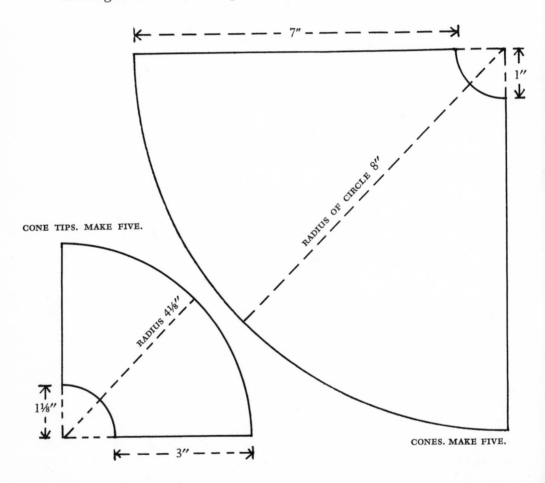

CONE TIPS. MAKE FIVE.

RADIUS 4⅛″

RADIUS OF CIRCLE 8″

1⅛″

3″

7″

1″

CONES. MAKE FIVE.

Cement tips onto the cut cones at the narrow end of the cone. Now form the five cones by overlapping the straight edges on each one and cementing together.

Make 1″ cuts around bottom edges of every cone. Fold back these cut edges and, beginning at bottom edge of *piñata* opening, paste the five cones in a straight line around the wet *piñata* form. Allow form to dry and deflate balloon. Attach harness by tying rope securely around the

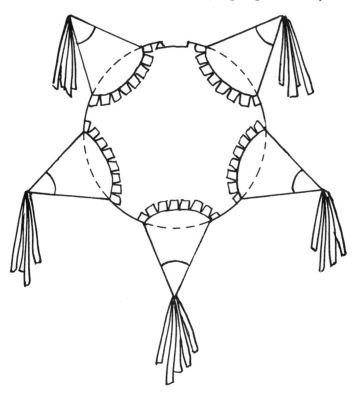

Star form showing tassels on cones and cones attached to *piñata* form

fullest part of the form. Use masking tape to secure rope. Be sure to leave loop in end of harness, near *piñata* opening, so that the suspension rope may be tied to it.

Decorate *piñata* form by applying white tissue ruffling from base of aluminum cone tips to base of cones. Apply one row of magenta ruffling, and fill in remaining areas of *piñata* form with blue tissue ruffling. To make tassels cut one sheet of blue and one sheet of white tissue paper into strips, ¼" x 6". Divide into five equal bunches, composed of both blue and white strips, and staple one bunch to every cone tip.

Approximate size: 23" across.

WITCH

You will need:

    1 egg-shaped balloon that can be inflated to 15″
    newspaper strips
    liquid starch or paste
    4 sheets of black tissue paper, 20″ x 30″, or 1 package of black
        crepe paper, 20″ x 7½″
    1 sheet of white tissue paper, 20″ x 30″
    1 sheet of orange tissue paper, 20″ x 30″
    1 sheet of black construction paper, 12″ x 18″
    1 scrap of red construction paper
    1 scrap of grey construction paper
    1 piece of aluminum foil, 4″ x 4″
    Rubber cement
    10 feet of hemp rope
    masking tape

Inflate balloon to 15″ and tie. Allow a 3 x 3″ uncovered area at top of balloon for *piñata* opening. Apply four layers of newspaper strips which have been dipped in starch or paste to the balance of the form. Allow form to dry. Deflate balloon.

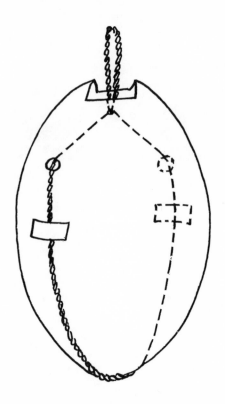

Witch form showing rope harness encircling *piñata,* rope inserted through holes in sides and brought up through the top

Punch two small holes, one on each side of *piñata* form, about 7″ down from top. Attach rope harness by encircling form from bottom upward to the small holes in the sides. Masking tape may be used to secure the rope to the form. Insert ends of rope through holes and bring rope out through the uncovered area at top. Be sure to make a sturdy loop so that the suspension rope may be attached.

Beginning at area allowed for *piñata* opening, apply nine or ten rows of white ruffling. Cover remainder of *piñata* with black ruffling.

Using pattern shown in diagram, cut nose of grey paper. Cement straight edges together. Make ¼″ cuts at bottom of nose cone. Bend the cut portions back, apply rubber cement to them, and attach the nose to *piñata* form 2½″ down from opening.

Using pattern shown in diagram, cut eyes of black construction paper and mouth of red paper. Cement eyes ½″ from center of nose. Cement mouth on form 1½″ beneath nose.

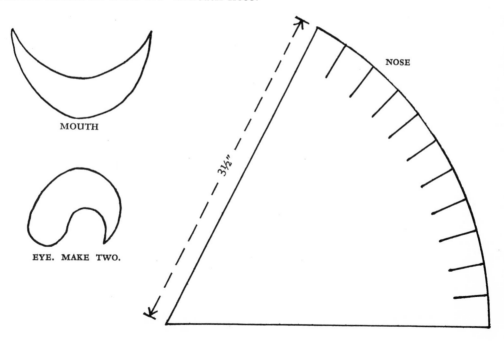

MOUTH

EYE. MAKE TWO.

3½″

NOSE

WITCH

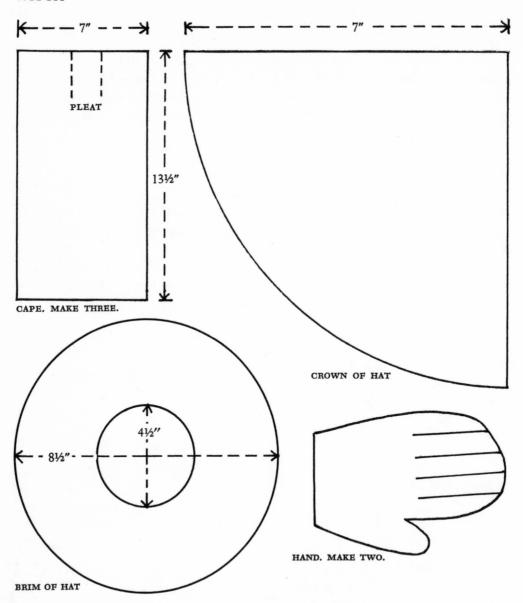

7"

PLEAT

13½"

CAPE. MAKE THREE.

7"

CROWN OF HAT

8½" 4½"

BRIM OF HAT

HAND. MAKE TWO.

Cut three cape pieces as shown in diagram (each piece to be 13½″ x 7″) and make 1″ pleats at top of each 7″ side. Secure pleats with staple or tape. Cement cape pieces at base of white ruffling, one piece at the back and one piece at each side.

Cut hands from aluminum foil and cement inside (at lower center) of cape pieces.

Cut hair from orange paper, using pattern in diagram. Fold paper as shown and make ⅛″ cuts to within 1 inch of fold.

Following pattern in diagram, cut crown and brim of hat from black construction paper. Cement straight edges of crown together. Make ¼″ cuts at bottom edge of crown and cement inside brim (See diagram). With paste or rubber cement attach hair inside hat at back and sides.

Place hat on witch and bring rope of harness up through cone tip of hat.

Approximate size: 23″ high.

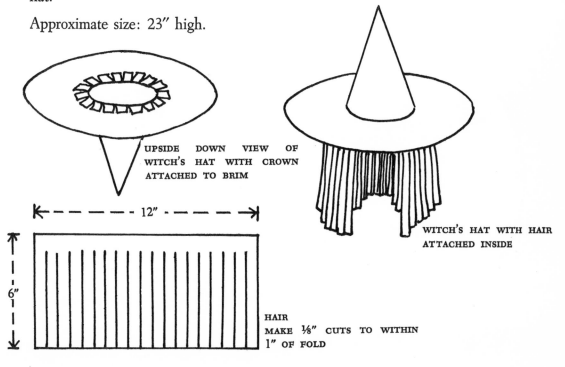

UPSIDE DOWN VIEW OF WITCH'S HAT WITH CROWN ATTACHED TO BRIM

WITCH'S HAT WITH HAIR ATTACHED INSIDE

HAIR
MAKE ⅛″ CUTS TO WITHIN 1″ OF FOLD

GLOSSARY AND PRONUNCIATION GUIDE

bolero	(bo-LAY-ro) *Sp*. An Andalusian dance.
Cuaresma	(kwah-REHS-mah) *Sp*. The Lenten season.
Cyclops	(SI-klops) In Greek mythology one of a race of giants having one eye in the middle of the forehead.
festas	(FEHS-tahs) *It*. Holidays or feast days.
fiestas	(fee-EHS-tahs) *Sp*. Holidays or feast days.
flamenco	(flah-MENG-ko) *Sp*. A dance. The flamingo.
huaraches	(wah-RAH-chehs) *Sp*. Loose sandals or slippers.
Lent	The period (forty days, not including Sundays) before Easter.
Moors	The people of Morocco, North Africa
nacimiento	(nah-see-mee-EHN-to or nah-thee-mee-EHN-to) *Sp*. Scene representing the nativity. A creche.
olla	(O-yah or OL-yah) *Sp*. Kettle; vessel; pot.
padre	(PAH-dreh or PAH-threh) *Sp*. Father; priest; monk
papier-mâché	(PAY-per ma-SHAY) From the French, but in common usage in English, meaning a hard substance made of paper pulp mixed with sizing, rosin, etc.
pascua	(PAHS-quah) *Sp*. Originally Passover; now any of the church holidays.
Pascua de Cuaresma	(PAHS-quah day kwah-REHS-mah) *Sp*. The Lenten Season.
pentolaccia	(pen-to-LAH-chah) *It*. Game played in Tuscany, Italy.
pesos	(PAY-SOS) *Sp*. Money, currency, dollars. The monetary unit of several Spanish speaking countries.
pigna	(PEEN-yah) *It*. Pine cone. A cone-shaped bunch of grapes. The word has other meanings also in architecture and engineering.

pignatta	(peen-YAH-tah) *It.* The clay pot used in the game where a blindfolded player breaks the pot to release the treats it holds.
piñata	(peen-YAH-tah) *Sp.* The game, and the decorated container used in the game, where a blindfolded player breaks the container to release the treats with which it is filled.
posada	(pos-SAH-dah or po-SAH-thah) *Sp.* Inn or shelter.
Posadas	(po-SAH-dahs or po-SAH-thahs) *Sp.* Pageants enacted in Mexico from the sixteenth to the twenty-fourth of December, symbolizing the struggle of the Holy Family to find shelter.
Renaissance	(ren-a-SAHNCE) A transitional period (fourteenth-sixteenth centuries) in Europe marked by a vigorous revival of interest in literature and the arts.
tejocotes	(tay-ho-KO-tehs) *Sp.* Fruit somewhat like the wild plum.
zarabanda	(sahr-a-BAHN-dah) *Sp.* A dance. The saraband.